Christian pilgrims share a common destination, a common hope; ideally, we share a common life. With so much in common, struggling to tread the same narrow path; we're a peculiar lot, often traveling diverse paths, far and wide, in order to find that one thing needful. Neither here nor there, this most precious treasure is to be found enshrined in a place much deeper than that.

It may seem that you can't get there from here. Jean Hoefling's _Journey to God_ helps to guide us to that place, the same place where even Saints have trod, shining a light toward that fulfilling destiny that is, truth be told, a deep breath and a heartbeat away.

> \- **Fr. Joseph David Huneycutt**
> Author of _One Flew Over the Onion Dome_ and _Defeating Sin_ (Regina Orthodox Press)

Jean Hoefling's _Journey to God_ is a wonderful sharing of some of her most important spiritual journeys, written with love and humor, and at times, an almost painful honesty. In sharing her life, she also reminds us that not every journey is successful – at first glance. Yet even apparent failures provide lessons that enrich us in the end.

> \- **Fr. Seraphim Gisetti**
> Pastor, St. John Chrystostom Mission, Golden, Colorado

Journey to God is an engaging spiritual travelogue, a quest for deeper spiritual understanding and expression… Jean pulls us into the eternal moment of life with the saints as she encounters the power and love of the modern St. John of San Francisco. She will have you in hysterics over her attempt to become a hesychast on silent retreat. These tales, told with honesty, vulnerability and seasoned with a healthy dose of humor, are sure to inspire and edify the reader.

> \- **Monk Martin**

Monastery of St. John of Shanghai and San Francisco

You do not have to be Orthodox to discover that Jean Hoefling has a contagious passion for God. These well-written accounts of pilgrimage should ignite the spiritual hunger of anyone who dares to press beyond the ordinary into the extraordinary.

- **Douglas Groothius**
   Professor of Philosophy at Denver Seminary and author of *On Jesus* (Wadsworth)

Jean Hoefling can be reached at:
jeanhoefling@hotmail.com.

JOURNEY TO GOD

ISBN 978-1-928653-38-7

Regina Orthodox Press
PO Box 5288
Salisbury MA 01952

reginaorthodoxpress.com

Journey to God:

How I Made a Pilgrimage to the Heart of Orthodoxy (Without Traveling Very Far) and Found Peace, Love and Stillness

by

Jean Hoefling

You cannot take all luggage with you on all journeys; on one journey even your right hand and your right eye may be among the things you have to leave behind.

C.S. Lewis

for Tim

But one man loved the pilgrim soul in you.
And loved the sorrows of your changing face.

William Butler Yeats

Introduction

A child drops a pebble into the stillness of a pond, its watery likeness reflecting the sky and clouds overhead. The pebble creates a supple implosion as it strikes the surface of the glassy liquid and sinks beneath the water line; contact between the two mediums radiates outward in broad, concentric waves. Tiny ridges and hollows emerge as a kaleidoscope that transforms the placid surface into thousands of minute mirrors, reflecting bright stabs of sunlight, the fragment of a bird in flight, the child's face in corrugated, undulating slivers. The circular waves brim with movement and rhythm, light and shadow.

So it is when God's energy collides compellingly with the smooth complacency of the human soul; His impact effecting more worthy expressions of person-hood than the soul left to itself. Responding to this divine disturbance, then, necessitates grace, as well as hard, unapplauded spiritual work rendered in humility out of the everyday routine that is the bulk of our lives.

That hard spiritual work thrives in the slog of consistent routine. Yet sometimes variety is called for to gain fresh perspective on the real state of one's spiritual life. Then getting out is in order – pilgrimage, holy journey – to places God has uniquely marked, provided to offer a different point of view.

Etymology of the word *holy* suggests health and wholeness – completion. Just how far one may still be from that wholeness can be brought out with surprising ease through the complexities and vulnerabilities such a journey entails.

Despite the many benefits of pilgrimage, holy journey to certain religious sites is never required of Christians, contrary to the traditions found in some religions. The center of the Christian faith is not geographical. Though Jerusalem is indeed a holy Christian city, not even there do we find the center of the Christian faith. That center is reserved for the human heart. St. Jerome reminded fourth century Christians captivated by the new fad of pilgrimage to the Holy Land: "Access to the courts of heaven is as easy from Britain as it is from Jerusalem."

Access to the courts of heaven. Some understand this better than others. According to tradition, the Desert Father Sarapion the Sindonite was a self-described wanderer. On pilgrimage to Rome he came across a renowned recluse who never left one small room. When asked why she was "just sitting there", the holy woman answered, "I'm not sitting; I'm on a journey." She understood what few of us do; the most fundamental pilgrimage is an inner journey to God, and with God. All the travel in the world won't make up for a spiritual vacuum.

But it's possible that the recluse hadn't always cloistered herself within four walls. Once she might have been a beginner like the rest of us. I envy her spiritual verve, but for the time being I seem to need the periodic revival that pilgrimage offers, the atmosphere when I'm out that's different than what I extract from prayer and reflection in my own living room. It seems to matter where I put myself geographically. The atmosphere near relics of a renowned saint is different than the one in front of my own icons at home. The Divine Liturgy conducted deep in the monastic night does something for me – different, not better or worse – than services in my home parish.

Until about a decade ago, it had not occurred to me to "go on pilgrimage" as a spiritual exercise. The religious tradition I had known since childhood had never challenged me to travel very far outside my Bible for help. I couldn't have articulated it because I had nothing to compare it to, but it seems faith was primarily a state of belief determined by my response to the Scriptures. It was largely mental in content. Of course there were the times I'd stand dumbfounded just below timberline while a meadow of wildflowers screamed God into my eyes. This was a holy journey all its own. But visits to overtly religious sites – monasteries, saint's shrines, holy wells or relics – was not part of my thinking.

If I thought about pilgrimage at all, Chaucer's lusty cast on the road to Canterbury might come to mind. Or more darkly, the penitential travels of Count Fulk the Black, who slogged in shackles three round trips from France to Jerusalem – a total of 15,000 miles – for such admittedly grave offenses as the burning of monasteries and the murder of his own wife. Like most moderns, this focus on boisterous tourist outings or demonstrations of radical penance seemed unnecessary to me.

I'm glad I finally set out on some of these unnecessary, outdated journeys. It took getting out to discover I'd needed them all along, just as it took the medieval pilgrim Anselmo Adorno several arduous trips to Jerusalem from points in Western Europe to conclude that "everything that is in this world changes and crumbles away." We may use pilgrimage to conclude both; this world is passing away and offers relatively little compared to the one to come. Yet Christ has blessed and sanctified the present world as a learning link to that coming one. Either way, we win by going.

With or without the Count's bare feet and hair shirt, I'm finding that pilgrimage can be a package for ongoing repentance. Repentance has its roots in something stronger than feeling sorry for past deeds. The best definitions imply action; walking in the opposite direction; reweighing priorities. Walking thousands of miles in shackles is not required for this weighing-in, but something else may be.

So I've gone, to find out what that something else might be. Like millions of people before me, I've set out assuming I'd discover things *there*, which I did. More importantly, what I gathered *there* stays *here*, within the place we call the soul, completing the cycle of genuine pilgrimage the Roman recluse understood.

On pilgrimage, God has wooed me toward this repentance through the force of the differences to daily life I've encountered – the intensity of monastic worship, a fragment of humble relic, the surreal landscape of loneliness, a nun's gentle admonition, even an elbow of moon among silvered clouds on an eerie desert night that jolted me into weeping wonder at His keen, inescapable presence. I have run from such moments, in terror of the holy Lover behind them. And I have walked toward them as well, pilgrim staff in hand.

The reader who indulges me in the following chapters should understand that I am a spiritual kindergartner. Kindergartners don't travel far from home, but venture out for a few hours a day to learn their alphabet and play well with others. Despite the riches of the ancient Orthodox Church to guide me, I confess to a limited understanding of how the Christian life is to be "done", on or off pilgrimage.

I usually don't understand how God works, only that He does. The complexities of life tend to overwhelm me. I wander around with a little note pinned to my shirt: "Jeanie is lost; please take her home." Until I can get around without the note – assuming that happens before I finally go to my ultimate Home – I have tried to keep an unpretentious periphery around the subject of pilgrimage, traveling not far beyond the horizon outside my playroom window.

In the end, many of us will go on pilgrimage because we are compelled, perhaps driven by the subconscious wanderlust to return to that womb of wholeness our race once had with God in Eden. Until Paradise is open to us again, we continue to strain through the thorny barricade of our banishment to catch a glimpse of our ultimate locus of longing, that holy thing lost – the Tree of Life – the deep heart of God. The holy places provided by the Church may ease our longing along the way.

So since we must, then let us go – in repentance and to the glory of God.

Journey to God

CHAPTER 1: Origins

Upon Thee have I leaned from my birth.
Psalms 71:6

Depending on one's doctrinal viewpoint, it's possible that I've been a Christian all my life. As a newborn, my parents dedicated me to God, a non-liturgical Protestant compromise with the more ancient Christian tradition of infant baptism. Before the congregation in a stately old Baptist church, my parents held their firstborn infant, heralding their pride through the wide, embracing smile of my father. My mother would have been a little breathless with old fears, hardly daring joy. Another baby had been stillborn with many abnormalities early in their marriage. The shock seems to have jolted their young bodies into eight years of agonizing infertility.

The red haired child they held on that morning of dedication was plump and perfect, destined for life. The minister would have blessed the baby and admonished all parents present to raise their children in the fear of the Lord. It was the last time my parents participated in this ritual; the three siblings that followed me were never dedicated. My hunch is that I came along just under the wire, before the Johnsons became Bohemian intellectuals whose friends would not have approved of innocent children being offered up to archaic notions of deity. I applaud their decision to stay in the Baptist church throughout the Bohemian years while many of their friends turned aside in disillusionment from the faith of their fathers.

I was not only destined for life, but captivated early in Christian consciousness. As a preschooler rustling in blue organdy, a large painted mural on the wall of my Sunday school room riveted me; a painting of

Christ outside the tomb among the angels just after His resurrection. Glorious in cloud-white robes, the risen One exuded something from that mural that made me shiver in my pin curls. With a sensation I later associated with roller coasters, my throat would constrict and my lower back begin to ache as I stared at the scars in His hands and between the straps of His sandals. I was weak with awe at this Jesus who had been cold and dead – completely, the Bible said – but who had returned to breath on an Easter morning of robin's egg skies and milky lilies. And with a child's sky-clear instincts, I believed.

For some, a preschooler's aching sacrum wouldn't be enough to render her Christian. There's a whole school of thought to the effect that the awed toddler in organdy wouldn't *really* have "become a Christian" until the afternoon in the middle of second grade when she knelt by her rumpled trundle bed and prayed the "sinner's prayer" dear to every Baptist. With Jesus "in her heart" and "the day and the hour" of conversion tucked safely within the folds of memory, Jeanie Johnson became an official Christian *that* day.

But she was a mere child at the time, still others would argue, and couldn't have understood the "full implications" of the Gospel, despite Christ's assertion that heaven is heavily populated by children, the mentally disabled and other innocent, guileless ones. According to this theory, I wouldn't have been an official Christian until a particular Sunday morning as a young teenager during the invitational hymn at the end of service. Mid-hymn, Someone I understood to be the Holy Spirit showed up in my pew under the guise of an orb of white-hot conviction in my solar plexus. The message was clear: in keeping with the traditions of our church I was to "go forward" and publicly commit my life to

Christ. As much as I appreciated the One from the wall mural with punctured hands, I recoiled at the thought of such a public display of affiliation with Him, or anyone else for that matter.

Protests were met with benevolent silence throughout the tempestuous week that followed as I tried valiantly to ditch the orb. God would have His way. By the following Sunday I was transformed, Jonah-like, from a self-conscious adolescent in knee socks to a steely-eyed aspirant ready to hoist my cross. I'd have done anything at that point to escape the agony in my solar plexus. Head tingling with hyperventilation, I held fast to my grandmother's hand and stepped up to face the pastor and people, come what may.

What came was the desire to be baptized. The following Easter my body was robed in white and immersed backward in the large baptistery that held a prominent place at the front of our sanctuary. Within the competent arms of the Reverend D. Raymond Parry, I savored the crystal water of regeneration – a death unto life – as the names of Father, Son and Holy Spirit were invoked over my head. It doesn't get any better than baptism, and finally there ought to be something in this very physical story of aching, churning, tingling body parts to satisfy almost everyone.

The early Christians understood that baptism compelled a complete change of life and worldview, and the newly illumined were carefully nurtured to that end. But no one spoke to me of changed worldviews. In the aftermath of that Easter day, I dislodged only the pitfalls of adolescence, evading my confusion through adrenaline-powered thespian pursuits or endless crushes on elusive, shaggy-haired boys from the halls at school. In the lulls, I would implode emotionally on long brooding walks in the woods behind our house. Sick about God, life and ninety-five other things, I was a stranger to the tiny innocent in blue organdy left behind in those earlier days of lucid inner sight.

By God's grace my buffeted faith survived into college, where I discovered Lordship Decisions, memorized entire chapters of the Bible, hiked into the mountains alone to pray under the stars, and offered my coat to a hollow-eyed runaway. These hopeful expressions of Christian piety should satisfy the lingering few who believe, quite rightly, that a Christian need walk out faith in obvious ways for that faith to be valid.

But the story of anyone's spiritual journey is like every trip to the grocery store: there's always one thing you forgot to pick up. Years into adulthood I took the step of Chrismation, a confirmation rite dating from the time of the apostles that aligned me in belief and worship to the Orthodox Church. On the day I received slick crosses of holy oil on my forehead, hands and feet, I sensed profoundly that I was being grafted into the universal Church in a way I hadn't been a participant before. I have never regretted my decision.

For several years after that, I was like a baby who only has eyes for her mother. My zeal for all things Byzantine ranged from the sublime to the annoying; for me, nothing existed that didn't relate to the Church. Ironically, this intense preoccupation is exactly what led me to more fully appreciate the background that had brought me to Orthodoxy in the first place. The faith that had been cultivated from my infancy still manifested itself continually in my prayers and outlook, my constant God-consciousness. I had given up nothing, only found a culmination for spiritual focus.

One skim-milk winter Sunday, I woke up craving contact with that church of my childhood, that building and those people that had woven thousands of threads into the tapestry of my life. I wanted to spend a couple of hours in worship with any who still attended that little church, to breath the air of that place, sing the hymns I still knew by heart and to dig my hands into the soil where my love for God had first germinated. I wondered if the resurrection mural was still at the back of the Sunday school room, and what it would feel like all these years later to stand next to the baptistery where God had regenerated me.

To visit Harvey Park Baptist Church, however, I'd have to forego a morning of elegant worship in my own parish, a jewel box of delights where senses and spirit are glutted each week with the extravagance of worship so glorious I sometimes fear I'll wake to discover it has all been a dream. I distinctly remember services at Harvey Park. They were nice – reverent even – but no jewelry box. I would feel the sting of that lack, but that would be part of the reason for it all – returning to what I'd known to appreciate what I had. And who was I to disdain the spirit of the place that had brought me to faith so long ago?

The church parking lot had miraculously shrunk over the years, the wont of so many props left on the set of childhood's drama, from entire houses, to play grounds, to kindergarten teachers. Pulling into a parking place that morning triggered memories of our family consistently arriving late to church. And it wasn't just church; the six of us managed to arrive for almost everything appallingly late, something wedding ushers frown heavily on, I can tell you. Old report cards from early grade school tally a generous number of tardy marks. This alternative relationship with time must have been part of the Bohemian intellectual worldview.

I had despised being late, but would bravely turn the knob on my Sunday school classroom door anyway, in the dutiful manner of girls of my birth order. More shy and less beholden to her elders than I, my sister routinely hid in the foyer coat closet until Sunday school was over, wrapping Mrs. Schmoker's black gabardine coat around her and hoping pigeon-toed feet in Mary Janes wouldn't be detected. I don't even want to know where my brothers were.

The nice couple that greeted me at the door that morning had been at Harvey Park since about the time I'd been in middle school. They didn't remember me, or any of my siblings. A few granted that they recalled my reserved mother, the closet beatnik who had so cleverly disguised herself as an unassuming back row Baptist over the years. A flicker of memory appeared in the eyes of one old man regarding my father, who had sung lead tenor in the choir but was often enough in one of his Darwinist phases and might not show up at church for months, especially if he and his mother-in-law had been arguing about the existence of dinosaurs. I was relieved when Mr. Dunbar recognized me. He'd entertained the junior high Sunday school for years with drug horror stories out of his experience as a guidance counselor in a rough school district.

But the gang that couldn't recall my existence to save their souls practically threw confetti when I mentioned my grandparents – a beloved pipe-smoking grandfather and two grandmothers – each of whom had made their unforgettable splashes over the many years our extended family attended Harvey Park. Despite the blank drawn almost universally about me, these kind people were willing to receive me like a suitor receives his long-lost love, thanks to my genetic link to the grandparents. If I was good enough for Alice and Essie, I was good enough for them.

My paternal grandfather, possessing the wonderful old southern name of Freeman, had taken the job of church custodian after his retirement. On Saturday afternoons, my little brother would set sail across the linoleum atop an electric waxing buffer Grandpa pushed until every floor shone. Harvey Park Baptist never looked better than the years he had this job.

My paternal grandmother, "Mamaw" Essie-Bell, was a lively little Kentuckian, a leader on the deaconess board, serving up punch and sandwiches at every church wedding and funeral. She knitted "cancer pads" by the hundreds for foreign mission hospitals, and brought me with her to the nursing home to visit old Miss Cubbage, bedridden for years with "the palsy".

Mamaw Alice was more subdued, a bookish southern Victorian who had hopped freight trains at age 16 to attend Peabody College and had dabbled with a graduate degree before she found time to marry and have children in her 30's. She was an avid student of the Bible, and Harvey Park's favorite adult Sunday school teacher. Naturally gifted, Mamaw managed to make even the long and annoying parts of the Bible interesting, and her classes on eschatology were especially popular with the Baptists, who thrive on nailing down "the day and the hour" for everything from religious conversions to end times events. Reverend Parry had given her the cream of the classrooms – his wood-paneled office. There she held court every week in her blue tweed suit and silver wig, armed with an enormous Scofield Bible and pages of careful notes.

By the time I was a young teenager, my sister and I were both foregoing more youthful fare to join the adults for Mamaw's irresistible descriptions of life during the Great Tribulation, that final hellish phase of Earth's history before the return of Christ. Thanks to her vivid rendition of nightmare conditions on the planet during the plague of demon locusts in Revelation 9, I decided the Tribulation sounded like an exciting time in which to live, and told the teacher so. She feigned horror at such a notion, but deep down, I think she agreed.

A young child's earliest perceptions of religion are most relentless in their haunting power. Yet unsmudged by too much contact with life, experiences bypass the mind and are absorbed almost directly through the child's heart and nervous system. Pleasant, wholesome impressions about church speak to an instinct deep within children, who know intuitively that the atmosphere surrounding this entity we refer to as "God" ought to be ethereal, beautiful and safe.

My great emotional attachments about church services are all of that; happy, cozy images of the original "old sanctuary" at Harvey Park, a one-story red brick rectangle typical of the whirlwind of American post-war construction to accommodate burgeoning suburban populations. Tan metal folding chairs, plain linoleum floors, a baptistery hidden under a trap door in the floor and a small dais the preacher and choir might squeeze onto completed this temple of no-nonsense religion, a "sanctuary" in the loosest aesthetic sense.

But on Sunday mornings a small girl in a blue velveteen dress absorbed something else through the filter of an imagination fired on weekdays by visions of fairies and mermaids, carried over into heavenly themes on the weekend. The miracle was that into this cube of utilitarian Protestantism, strong Colorado sunshine sliced its way through long, pink stained glass windows in shafts of rose-tinted air that created an aura of rapture, transforming allegedly ordinary objects and people into a wonderland of soft pink happiness. I took this marvel completely for granted; church air was pretty, just as heaven air would be pretty.

My mother sat beside me in the tinted atmosphere, elegant and still in her sheath dress and pearls. Velvet-lined soup plates were passed down the rows while an organ played softly. Aglow with the rosy light, in veiled hats and white gloves, French twists and shirtwaists, patent leather and bow ties, the Baptists sang stirring hymns rich with Mighty Fortresses, Jordan's Stormy Banks and The Thunder of Thy Clarion. In the rarefied glow, our dignified Welsh pastor delivered subdued sermons quite uncharacteristic of more typical Baptist clergy. Life was good in the old sanctuary.

I was confused the year we left this secure and dream-like setting to stream into the luxurious *new* sanctuary that would accommodate our expanding community, as we had become the fastest-growing American Baptist congregation in the Denver area. The new sanctuary seemed vast, sporting shiny wooden pews, an impressive organ and a triangular white baptistery at the center of the dais, not hidden under a trap door like something out of a Dutch Resistance documentary. Stained glass windows now sported pink *and* blue squares and a large wooden cross graced the wall behind the pulpit with its fancy microphone. All these years later, it's still a nice-looking room that wouldn't offend anyone's sensibilities.

But I worried about the old sanctuary. I was sure its feelings were hurt, for in the transition to progress it had been cast aside, reassigned to lowly Sunday school space. This seemed impossible to my young mind; how could a sanctuary become a Sunday school? The dais was devoid of pulpit and organ, while the old tan folding chairs were assembled irreverently around tables instead of lined up in neat, worshipful rows. Abandoned and still, no human sounds cheered the hour of worship from that space. And the light of heaven filtered unnoticed into the emptiness.

On the morning of my pilgrimage, I stood in the doorway of the old sanctuary and remembered these impressions. Like the rest of childhood's geography, the room has dwarfed with time. It is currently rented to a group whose members conduct their services in Chinese. Where the choir once stood is a clutter of drums, keyboards and thick black cables – the accoutrements of contemporary Evangelical worship. Across jumbled rows of chairs, squares of the old rosy light slipped into the nap of a wrinkled red carpet, turning the air a hue that made me turn away.

I adjusted to the new sanctuary, where impressions continued to layer down their weekly strata. In that room for an hour each week until she went to college, the girl that few can remember lived and breathed in enough of God for Him to work Himself under her skin for life. Through the example of my elders, my mind recorded emphatically that God was worth dressing up for, being quiet for, bowing one's head for week after week.

Year after year I watched my mother pray the Lord's Prayer with head bowed. I learned this prayer, the Doxology, and Protestant hymns penned from the hearts of ardent Christians across the centuries, from Reformation Germany to the hollows of 19th century Appalachia. And I was made to understand that Communion was mysterious and outside the realm of children, something that would wait in the wings of that shrouded future day when I might be old enough to "understand".

Until then, I was to keep my hands to myself as the doily-lined silver trays of tiny wafers passed me by every first Sunday of the month. I can still hear the muffled shiver of glass against sterling silver as tiny goblets rattled in their compartmentalized trays, jiggling the precious mouthfuls of grape juice offered to the Baptists as a simple remembrance of Christ's death. I still have to stifle the urge to fold my hands and show a little respect whenever I catch a whiff of Concord grape juice.

On that day of pilgrimage I took my place in the pew near the front of the sanctuary where I'd sat the morning the Holy Spirit moved in for the kill. I had the memorable bench all to myself, for the sanctuary was more than half empty, dotted mostly with elderly people and a few families. In this pew, wedged between my grandmothers with their faint scent of powder and hand lotion, I had first strained to "really pay attention" to the minister's sermons, an achievement I made note of in my diary. There had been gum and mints to be mined from the bottom of grandma purses, and the fascination of watching those two precious ladies fiercely mark up their Bibles during the sermons.

I thought back to the years I was faced Sunday after relentless Sunday with the certainty that God and Christ were real, that there was a way to express that certainty in a public setting; this thing called "church" where people held certain common beliefs and tried to put those beliefs into practice. Church was a good thing – protective, ritualistic, pre-determined in its importance. And whether or not my father stayed home with *The Origin of Species* or had his ear to the ball game on the little gray radio, my mother got us to church. Snow storms that paralyzed more visible church members didn't phase her, sputtering through deadlocked streets in the white Corvair with four whining kids, the barest scent of the White Ginger cologne my father had brought her from Hawaii wafting from her calm profile. I credit my own steady church habits with my mother's wordless consistency. Habits forged in childhood die hard.

I never heard my mother speak of her own life with God. I never saw her reading the Bible. But she was in the second-to-last pew on the organ side every week. I was well into adulthood when she told me she continued to attend church to please her mother. She had confided that when Mamaw Alice died, she planned to stop going. But in the years after Alice Lewis finally did die – six months short of a century old – Ruth Johnson was still hard at it every week in the second-to-last pew.

"I keep thinking she can still see what I'm doing," she admitted with some bewilderment, as though astonished to discover she was not as free-spirited as she'd imagined. Heaven must have seemed uncomfortably close.

After the service – remarkably unaltered from the way my memory had recorded it – people moved into the fellowship hall for a reception for one of their own who'd turned fifty, complete with death-knell symbols like black balloons and the sort of aggressive birthday cake message about aging whose purpose I never quite understand. The awareness of my own exclusion, the handicap of too many years between that place and myself suddenly overwhelmed me. I followed a few women down a hall I'd walked hundreds of times so many years ago. I imagined that I was still that child, snug in my green tartan coat, an integral part of the bustling life of that squeaky-clean suburban church. Before I'd reached the end of the hall, I was ready to leave. Pilgrimage to the past can be lonely.

But I was still curious about something. The pastor had offered to let me see the "archives", a dozen photo albums put together by members over the years. I craved some tangible evidence that I wasn't like those people in old *Twilight Zone* episodes who fall into another dimension, fated to journey in their adult states back in time to their home towns and end up screaming in despair because even their parents don't recognize them.

In the first album was a picture taken from the back of the old sanctuary during a service in the early years. A very young Reverend Parry raised an arm for emphasis during one of his reasonable and well-modulated sermons. Strange, but the pulpit looked as high in this picture as I remember it being as a child. Another picture showed a ladies quartet, the singers festive in fur collars. One was Mrs. Wollen, who was young and pretty and played stirring civil rights ballads on her guitar during Vacation Bible School.

There were pictures of church dinners and picnics, of the laughing church clown Joe Pastine, hair heavy with Brylcreem, wearing a chef's apron and brandishing a platter of spaghetti and meatballs with theatrical flair. There was Mrs. Robinson, the classy Sunday school superintendent in her smooth chignon, squinting into the sun on a wedge of church lawn amidst a bevy of children, while many newly planted trees grew furiously in the background. Mrs. Robinson had her hand on the shoulder of one of my brothers, and in the first row my sister shaded her eyes from the sun. So we *had* existed. In vain I searched the faces of the other children's classes. That I was nowhere seemed odd, considering I was the only one who never ditched. Beyond the two siblings, not even the grandmothers were to be found in a single photo.

I closed the last album and was gathering my things when an elderly woman stepped into the office. Margaret Campbell Pitney introduced herself and expressed interest in the purpose of my visit. At my prompting, she reeled off her own life story, unselfconsciously recounting a lifetime with someone she'd met only minutes before.

Margaret had joined Harvey Park as a single parent in the late 60's. Sometime afterward she had been baptized, on Easter Sunday of the year 1970. A hot little explosion went off in my memory, the fragment of a 30-something woman with short, dark hair robed in white, climbing a set of stairs that ascended out of a dressing room up into the waters of the baptistery. The fragment emerged out of the dim memory of the morning of my own baptism when I had stood with pounding heart to watch someone else enter the water ahead of me. And I knew that this faint memory of feminine movement was Margaret Campbell Pitney.

Mrs. Pitney searched my face. Yes, she did remember a young girl with her in the dressing room that morning. I plied her for details, clues to the person I'd been. What was she *like*, that girl, that day? But like me, Margaret's wisp of that other-one-in-white was too weak to recall more. And no amount of obsession to retrieve insights from the day we were both brought to life in Christ would bring back anything else.

After that there was little left to say to Margaret Campbell Pitney, my compatriot in sacrament. I left the church and drove the few blocks to the little house where we lived until I was twelve. Designed by the renowned architect Cliff May, the house still retains vestiges of the "architectural integrity" my modern-thinking parents and their friends were so proud of as young couples.

Enormous maple trees now dwarf the proportions of the mid-century ranch frame. The once casually chic neighborhood deteriorated for years after we moved. But that day, I noticed signs of a revival in appreciation for the clean lines found on those few neighborhood blocks surrounded by a sea of standard brick ranch houses. Some of the Cliff Mays had fresh paint and neatened lawns, and the current owner of our house had xeroscaped the front yard, giving the place an artsy, updated look.

I heard dogs from within the house so kept my distance, my eye on the gate that led through to a bricked patio my father had built. He and my mother had turned that enclosure into a magical oasis outlined with plantings of delphinium and roses, with moss rose and California poppies that spread in lushness over salt-bleached driftwood; rock gardens and walls of blue morning glories, masses of day lilies and tall clumps of Colorado columbine above which Japanese candle lanterns glowed in orbs of magenta and emerald on summer evenings. And over it all, the dappled shade of the tall maples.

Into the beauty, a shadow had fallen in the form of a dream I had before I ever started school and that still recurs at regular intervals. In the dream I am running through the rooms of that house in darkness to secure the glass door that opens onto the patio. In panic I shake and turn the knob to assure it is locked against the *something* that hulks outside, in the dark among the maples. I am always a child in pajamas sick with fear, and there is no one to help.

The source of that dream is locked somewhere within. The solution is not lodged in a sidewalk crack, or under the tall ponderosa pine we once used as a clubhouse, or embedded in fairy rings in the grass. Yet when I return to stand in front of that house, my child instincts take over with their own ways and means and I find myself once again searching grass-tufted cracks in the sidewalk for clues as to why the emissaries of my subconscious still prowl the place.

In a stroll down the street, I came across the lot where an old barn had stood, out of which an ominous silhouette of bats had once trickled at dusk, convincing me the barn was haunted. There was the park with its shining lake, beside which a bank of yellow tulips had once bloomed every early May. And I still felt a trace of heartbreak from the day I misplaced my tattered baby blanket somewhere in a neighbor boy's yard as we played. I had clawed obsessively among the junipers until darkness chased me home. But that umbilical link with the earliest fog of infancy was lost forever, no matter how often I returned to the search.

I completed the ritual of the old neighborhood on the playground of the grade school, the site of an early sensation of competence as I flew on a circle of steel jungle-gym rings a medium-sized child could reach by stretching high on two old tires. The rings are worn glossy by generations of children's hands – my own hands – every fall and spring until the blisters opened and bled and my hands yellowed to callous. The burning and blood had been yearly passage to the thrill of unleashed movement in my small body as I pumped and soared while younger children looked on.

We forget how much our senses remember, how strong the traces of our early forays into what it is to be alive. My recurring dream at the patio door reminds me that the past pushes into the present whether I want it or not. That morning at the church I had caressed the pink windows in the old sanctuary, searched the floor of the cloakroom where my sister had hidden, smoothed my hand around doorknobs and stared into the waterless white baptistery. Finally I had run my fingers along an unyielding white wall in search of a chip of exposed blue paint from which to peel back the sky and two nail-marked hands.

I am not the first to make such tactile, wordless quests into childhood places of play, worship and learning. For some like myself, such rites of the imagination and memory seem essential to draw the threads of life together, to better live it as a whole. Each time I journey backward, I have the sense of being torn in parts within myself, snagged with an irrational wish that I could simultaneously be the child I was and the woman I am. This is only the soul's deep instinct that it was never meant to entirely leave behind the child body and outlook, past and present never meant to be so polarized. In a gesture of retrieval, some of us poke among shreds of reminiscence to retain what we once were, and vaguely still are, in a world sadly more adept at segmenting and separating than making complete.

At home I rummaged in a file containing old school awards, track ribbons and a heavily-stamped passport from my young adult life. The baptism certificate was there too, citing the exact date Margaret Campbell Pitney had mentioned. In the background, behind the careful penmanship of some past church secretary, Jesus strolled across a minty meadow trailed by clean white sheep, a tiny lamb secured across His shoulders. In contrast to this pretty document, I'd been hard pressed to obtain the barest testament on church stationery from a mystified young receptionist after my oldest son's baptism at the "rock-n-roll church" of his teens.

I am a benefactor of an outlook largely formed within a wedge of history when innocent articles like baptism certificates really meant something. Some combination of experiences and impressions, brain chemistry, twists of Providence, the surprising actions of God and maybe even cracks in the sidewalk intertwined among the neighborhood corridors of my small childhood world to cultivate the person I am today. I believe I am better for having put on patent leather with my family every Sunday morning, even if we were the last ones in the pews every time.

CHAPTER 2: Speak to Him Thou

Speak to Him thou for He hears, and Spirit with Spirit can meet—
Closer is He than breathing, and nearer than hands and feet.
Alfred Lord Tennyson

The Jesus Prayer: "Lord Jesus Christ, Have Mercy on Me"

The soaring peaks of the Northwest Territories surround the Koyukon people of Alaska. Constantly confronted with the mountains' grandeur, they are forbidden by long tradition to speak of the size of those peaks while looking at them. "Don't talk; your mouth is small," is their credo. This restraint of voice toward that which is more enduring than their own lives constantly exhorts the indigenous Alaskans to speak little and ponder much on things greater than themselves. It is an exercise in humility.

Like those massive mountains, it's possible the jury is still out as to whether the Jesus Prayer should be analyzed or discussed very much. A few holy ones over the centuries have spoken and written of it. Their words are steeped in humility and in the credibility of their righteous lives. They have the ring of authority. Those of us in the throes of learning the fundamentals of prayer will do well to remember that our mouths are still small, that when it comes to expounding on the Prayer, less is more.

The Russian classic *The Way of a Pilgrim* is one of the notable accounts of the Jesus Prayer in action. Artlessly and without apparent intent to manipulate the reader or exalt his own insight, the author was allegedly a 19th century homeless wanderer who learned to integrate the Jesus Prayer deeply into his consciousness. He prayed the Prayer literally thousands of times throughout every day and night. This example is the ultimate challenge to those who desire to "pray without ceasing".

Many others have found this to be the most basic function of the Jesus Prayer; as a means to connect with the heart of God throughout the days and nights of our lives. We may not pray into the thousands, but this prayer with Jesus at the heart is as near to each of us as our next breath, our next choice. God isn't counting; He wants only *that* we pray.

It was my own desperate, inner homeless person that led me to this ancient prayer. Inured by chronic starvation of the spirit, I was a lonely hobo prowling among bundles of rubbish in the alleys of religion, and ducking under bridges out of the rain. My Christian experience had come to a season of astonishing poverty, in which the familiar formulas of worship and of belief transposed to life, no longer gave me shelter.

At the time I discovered the Jesus Prayer, I am ashamed to say my prayer life consisted largely of clichéd variations on a theme: "Lord, I just come to you because I just want…" accompanied by many zealous imperatives that God must needs hear. "Just" was handy; it bought me time to think my way out of the panic that came over me when I prayed, generally with myself at the center of things. I spent an enormous amount of psychic energy fighting down that panic, and with it the growing awareness that my soul was a cluttered place full of much nonsense.

By God's grace I found the Jesus Prayer, the Prayer of the Heart, on the pages of Thomas Merton's *Contemplative Prayer.* It was short and direct, composed of seven compelling words that in the moment of my first reading held all of faith, all of eternity as they jumped off the page and burned their way into my heart. Here was Everyman's primordial wail, a prayer for the dead serious in its most compressed, expectant state, faith with its back to the wall, warm and pungent, poured out like myrrh. The rest of the book blurred. In my desperate state at that time, it should not have surprised me that I'd attach to something as vital as the Prayer.

My response was the way of the starving. I grabbed that prayer and chewed as though my life depended on it; oblivious to the splinter-charged deck chair I sat on, out on a steamy sea of bottle-green lawn in the humid August of the Midwest. The brave new Prayer felt good in my mouth, nourishing, medicinal. I poured it out in descant above the lower urgency of my heart's plea: *Please, I have nothing left.* I traveled for a few minutes into the Prayer, into the uncluttered appeal of the Name of Jesus Christ, connector of everything whole and fragmented, healed and ill.

Then I paused. The sky had not fallen on me for having indulged in Heaping Up Vain Repetitions As The Heathen Do, for speaking to God without inserting the word "just", or failing to add creative addendums to the seven words. Lightening had not struck for praying something recommended by a Catholic. And nothing less than complete sincerity pulsed from my heart with every utterance of the Prayer.

But as Oscar Wilde has noted: "Sincerity is a dangerous thing, and a great deal of it is absolutely fatal." I had apparently sat long enough with my sincerity when a gray halo of mosquitoes swarmed up in frenzied blood lust from our nearby pond, emerald with its choke of algae. At their attack my concentration scattered like a flock of weightless birds and I ran for cover. Inside the screened porch, I grieved that God's creatures have so little refinement in the face of holy doings.

Thus began my love affair with the Jesus Prayer, that stunning, lilting language of the heavens, that delectable first kiss. It was my *Amen* at the sight of every gingery sunset, every hayfield polished with moonlight. It was all my praise, entreaty and lament, precious as a mother mode. Typical of the blush of first love, my cerebral cortex was not particularly connected to this new object of adoration. The words *Jesus Christ* were straightforward enough, and *me* was a favorite word too. But the meaning of *mercy* in the context of this prayer eluded me. After all, hadn't Jesus already shown His mercy on the cross all those centuries ago? Why would we keep asking for more?

For the time being though, my gut trusted the Prayer. I simply *liked* it. To not "understand" was part of the romance. Later I remembered that the Psalms and Gospels are full of it. It had taken Thomas Merton's little book to make this keening of the homeless, blind and outcast, my own. I didn't know then that it would both break and heal my heart, and change me forever.

The Jesus Prayer was a godsend at a crucial time, fortifying me to emerge from my dark night of the soul. Life seems to have felt an awful lot like Kira's failed-escape-across-the-frozen-Latvian-border in *We the Living*. I hadn't been shot by any border guards yet, but kept sensing it might be just over the next snowdrift. The Jesus Prayer became my ticket across that frozen border. It became a prayer of quest.

I started slipping away from my family's evangelical church every other Sunday, across the green border from Illinois into Wisconsin to worship at an Episcopalian church that looked quaintly like one Jane Austen might have liked. There, my sponge-like heart soaked up "empty ritual" from the Book of Common Prayer, bearing its deliciously unsolved liturgical resonance to my fundamentalist ears. I lost myself in the allegedly meaningless repetitions droned slipshod in the pews of this smoky, waxy den of empty ritual. This pilgrimage into the vast liturgical unknown rendered me almost giddy. *Forward* is the state motto of Wisconsin; I believed I was living a metaphor on those Wisconsin Sundays as I crossed the border.

The Wisconsin priest was the soul of kindness. He talked about Real Presence, patiently mentored my question, and with many friendly nods and smiles behaved as though violent inner revolutions of the sort I was fighting were as standard as making oneself a ham sandwich at lunchtime. I was on a path toward a liturgical world view that would eventually deposit me in the center of Eastern Orthodox spirituality.

It was nobody's fault that I no longer connected with the religious tradition I had always known. Many Protestants never step into a liturgical church or say the Jesus Prayer and live vibrant lives. But I very clearly wasn't one of them. I had become the curmudgeon at any friendly gathering, hacking off great chunks of Christendom for closer scrutiny. I got alarmed stares and smiles quivering with panic. Eventually, I shut up.

Typical of any other crush, ardent fascination with my new toys turned out to be insufficient to the task. Eventually, the intensity of what was embedded in seven little words demanded something like guidance. I dreamed of a kindly, bearded elder. I visualized a dozen like-minded souls sprinting up my front walk waving banners: "We too want to contemplate Christ in the Jesus Prayer!"

The proverbial winds of adversity blew into my life. How easily the strain of circumstances scattered the seed of my new prayer effort before it could firmly take root in my heart and understanding. I floundered, doubted, began doing a lot with the word "just" again. The Jesus Prayer, innocent as a newborn lamb, lay bleating outside my heart.

The *mistral* of that year died away. We moved to another state where I met people who not only knew of the Jesus Prayer, but also prayed it. I attended a few services at their Eastern Orthodox parish. There, even the people in the icons mounted on the walls held knotted prayer ropes made of black wool. I learned that the prayer rope is a tool something like a rosary, used in many religious traditions to harness concentration and to gauge prayers. Chrismation a year later completed one pilgrim ramble, and poised me to begin another.

I returned to the Prayer, only to discover that the glow of exhilaration I'd had months before was gone, the honeymoon over. Undaunted, I bought a prayer rope of my own, knotted by monks in a Michigan monastery. It consisted of thirty-three muscular black yarn bumps, one for each year of Christ's life, topped off with a tear tassel to mop up the fruits of contrition over sin.

Despite the tactile aid of the rope, with every repetition of the Prayer I felt like an Amazonian capybara slipping unawares for a swim into piranha-invested waters. Compulsions to jump up and do almost anything ripped constantly at my attention, devouring my drive to pray, stripping my motivation to bones. Worse, as the golden mists of novelty burned off forever, something cruel and insidious began to resist the Prayer with a great deal of muscle and machismo. "Real Men Don't Do No Crazy Prayer" became this goon's mantra day and night as he negated the Name of Jesus, scoffed at mercy, and mocked my earnestness.

Like staring up at Mount Everest from base camp fasting and barefoot, every movement of my thumb across each black knot had become a hurdle of

Himilayan proportions. What I'd hoped would transform me, I now dreaded. I was tempted to dismiss the whole experiment; maybe it really was Crazy Prayer. I rationalized: *I'm not the contemplative type. This goes against my gregarious grain. What was wrong with the "just" prayers after all?*

I was secretly relieved when I lost the prayer rope. To this day it lies deep within the fourth dimension between the box spring and mattress of my bed, in company with many vanished earrings and myriad pieces of alarm clocks obliterated under my crazed morning hand-thrashing over the years. There is no retrieving these items, ever.

For a long time, I stayed away from prayer ropes. They seemed hopelessly long, like the Nile, full of submerged crocodiles. So it was on a whim that I picked up a free plastic rosary while visiting a friend's Catholic church – pure Providence in such a simple thing. The rosary's silky white beads glowed slick and quick in the dark, radiating a pale green charm at bedtime. My fingers discovered they didn't have to dig for every knot as they had on the prayer rope, and each smooth oval bead was separated from its fellows by a short expanse of string. This gave a body time to catch her breath before moving on to the next *Our Father*, *Hail Mary*, or Station of the Cross.

About that time a friend spontaneously offered me a prayer rope he had knotted himself. It was a genuine big-girl rope; one hundred maroon knots graced with an enormous tear tassel. I was seen everywhere with it, flashing it around like a five-carat engagement ring. During the lengthening, greening days of that Lent I began to move cautiously over the soft red knots. It was during that Lent that the Prayer finally took hold, got under my skin and began to change me.

My mentor in this was the gray bearded elder I had often longed for, discovered in the pages of his writings, *Wounded by Love*. This contemporary Greek monk, Elder Porphyrios, had such a surprisingly jolly, joyful attitude toward the Jesus Prayer – as well as everything else, it seemed – that I couldn't resist giving up the angst I'd held onto for so long.

Force is not the way to acquire prayer. Pray without calculations, without ulterior motives. The prayer should not be said as a chore. Coercion may provoke a reaction within us and be harmful. It's not necessary to concentrate particularly to say the prayer. You don't need any effort when you're filled with divine love. You can say the prayer gently, without straining and without contortion wherever you happen to be. If your soul repeats with worship and adoration the seven words, *Lord Jesus Christ, have mercy on me*, it never can have enough. They are insatiable words! Repeat them all your life. There is such life-giving sap hidden within them! When you lose the divine grace, don't do anything. Continue your life and your struggle simply and normally until, without anxiety, you will be filled again with love and longing for Christ.[1]

My view of the heretofore mysterious word *mercy* was also changing. It was moving away from the stereotypical notion many Western people entertain of the word; to view oneself as a prisoner groveling for acquittal before a stern judge. In Greek, the word for

[1] Elder Porphyrios, *Wounded by Love* (Evia, Greece: Denise Harvey, 2005), pp. 120, 122

mercy is linguistically related to the one for *olive oil*, used in ancient times as a soothing and healing agent on wounds. This hopeful and humane concept of mercy is graphically illustrated in the Biblical story of the Good Samaritan, in which the ethnically unclean Samaritan massaged healing oils into the wounds of the Israelite who "fell among robbers."

We are all as desperate as the man who fell among those who desired only to deconstruct his existence. We lie bleeding and abandoned by a world unable to heal us spiritually or penetrate the deepest recesses of our souls. It is barely conceivable to most of us that Christ, Himself broken by the Cross, bends endlessly in tears over His assaulted ones, fighting to the death for their lives on a lonely road that swarms with treachery.

A lifetime after the first warm wind of God blew through my childish heart, years after I first began to pray the Jesus Prayer, I am still stiff with many wounds, still bleeding in places. I am sometimes circled in warmth, sometimes cold and listless in my pain. I have to struggle into God's presence every time I pick up a prayer rope and say the Name. When I persist, I warm to the Prayer. Then, the childlike joy of the Elder does come. So I persevere, drawing warmth into the chill places, cool elixir into the inflamed ones. He moves like medicine in my blood.

According to St. Ignatius, "to try to pray without ceasing is a hidden martyrdom." Prayer is a way through death in order to find life. It can be heavy with effort; Christ did promise a cross. Or with pride, for my soul is ungainly. But for those who will bear the Name on their lips and in their hearts, its absorption into the heart's deep places will one day bloom full. Then, the One within the Prayer will become the morning glory.

Journey to God

CHAPTER 3: The Journey's the Thing

First of all, you must learn to sit with yourself and to face boredom, drawing all the possible conclusions.
Bishop Anthony Bloom

I'd been Orthodox a couple of years, but had the nagging sense I was missing something. It came to me finally after running through a list of Orthodox embellishments: I had yet to view a genuine reliquary or the incorrupt body of a saint. It was a state of affairs I found wanting. The veneration of relics has an earthy history; early Christians received the Eucharist over the graves of their martyred fellows. Despite peoples' abuses of relics in times past, they continue to serve as object lessons for important Christian theology, even in these dissolute times. St. Justin Popovich explains the powerful theology embedded in the relic:

> In the God-Man, all matter has been set on a path toward Christ – the path of deification. Through its Divine and human existence in the Church, the human body, as matter, as substance is sanctified by the Holy Spirit and in this way participates in the life of the Trinity. Matter thus attains its transcendent, divine meaning and goal…its immortal joy in the God-Man… so that the entire man, the entire body, might be filled with God and with His miracle-working forces and powers. Thus we, in piously venerating the

Saints, also venerate the entire person, not separating the holy soul from the holy body."[2]

I, for one, am not willing to argue with such optimism. Inspired by St. Justin, I decided that relics were a perfect excuse for a pilgrimage. My daughter Adèle was scheduled to tour a college in Wichita, Kansas, renowned for its ballet program. I'd heard there was a collection of relics of apostles and saints the local bishop had made available in a small chapel inside the Cathedral of St. George. We could do both.

When I called, the dean of the cathedral reminded me that St. George's is not an official pilgrimage site of the Orthodox Church. He seemed a little confused at my excitement. This is the way of people who have probably made numerous pilgrimages across the collective bosoms of Greece, Russia and the Holy Land. But I hadn't. Kansas was good enough for me.

Though St. Justin's arguments seem perfectly reasonable, some people will still wonder why anyone would hover over the long-dead remains of *anyone*, holy or not. Christians are divided on this. Many Protestant traditions forbid fancy attentions toward deceased people, regarding this as idolatrous. Throwing the baby out with the bath water was standard Reformation procedure in dozens of areas as a reaction against medieval Catholic excesses. Yet I wonder if people have thought through their objections clearly. The same people that shun relics and icons can be found kneeling at the graves of deceased loved ones, clutching flowers

---

[2] Popovich, St. Justin. "Orthodox Tradition, Vol. VII, No. 1, p. 9"
The Place of Holy Relics in the Orthodox Church.
http://www.orthodoxphotos.com/Holy_Relics (21 June 2008)

and pouring out their hearts to persons clearly gone to their reward. It's a matter of perspective; human beings seem hard-wired to keep near us in some way that which has already gone over into the next world. This has nothing to do with ghosts or "spirit guides" or worshipping somebody besides God. We know deep down that the person we love lives on.

From an Orthodox perspective, to "venerate a relic" is to offer honor and respect from the heart and sometimes gestures of the body toward people who have already finished the race of faith in a manner the Church has blessed. We who remain want to thank them for their efforts and meditate on their lives and sanctity. The Church in her wisdom has determined which people especially merit this honor and it is these to whom we go for official veneration. We pray for them and ask their prayers. This reminds us of our connection of love with the entire Body of Christ, here and away.

"Matter is, in its innermost core, God-longing and Christ-longing," wrote St. Justin.[3] Though the soul of the saint is temporarily absent from the body, the physical atoms and molecules that make up that body still exist in some form on earth. This is hallowed matter awaiting the resurrection of all things. The hand of Mary Magdalene kept in a monastery on Mt. Athos is said to be soft and warm to the touch. It's as if heaven were saying, "Don't be sad. No one's actually *dead*; they're just pretending." The relic reminds us that death is not a dead end.

There may be many genuinely holy relics in the world not recognized by the Church. Should I venerate them all? A line must drawn somewhere or I might someday find myself kissing the hand of a Precious

---

[3] Ibid.

Moments porcelain figurine reasonably priced online at $250. So I venerate relics blessed by the Church, and leave the rest for others to decide about. Less is more. As my focus has narrowed, as I've chosen to study the world through one clear-paned window, it has expanded. The results of a sociology study on play and learning demonstrated that children without a fenced-in play area tended to huddle near the center, while children who were fenced in gravitated to the far corners of their limitations.

Relics grow on a person, like many things that begin awkwardly. I for one just *like* them, and I make no apologies. I haven't always been so enthusiastic. In my 20s, I lived for a while in Italy, where even the blandest curiosity about history and architecture will put one in contact with shrines and relics as a matter of course. My feelings were ambivalent about the fingers and splinters of femur I encountered on tourist outings in Florence and Rome.

In the *Capuchini* chapel in Rome, I didn't know whether to laugh or cry among the bones of 4000 monks on display in artistically designed dioramas in the six-room crypt. On one hand, heaven forbid that I should be taken for an idolater, or someone observed to be even *slightly* appreciating random bits of folks who may or may not have been all they are alleged to be. At the same time it seemed uncharitable to treat these human remains with the flippancy poked their direction by we out-of-towners. It wasn't that I'd ever established a conscious preference for religious sites devoid of human remains. It had simply never occurred to me that their presence might be advantageous.

Yet even then, a seed of awe was germinating in my heart, second thoughts about what was possible within the realm of faith. One particularly searing August afternoon stays in my memory. A friend and I had taken a bus to Siena, the rosy-gold medieval city at Tuscany's heart. As respite from the crowds in Piazza de Campo I'd escaped into the battlement-like church of San Domenico. There I wandered through the blissfully cool nave, accustomed by then to the characteristic scent of these old Italian churches; musty cloth, burning wax, cool stone permeated with centuries of incense residue. And exquisite silence.

But I wasn't prepared for what I encountered in my innocent stroll into a side chapel among shadows thrown by flickering prayer candles. There, ensconced reverently under glass as I remember, was the head of St. Catherine of Siena, who is Italy's patron saint. A shard or two of somebody in a closed reliquary at some random shrine was one thing, but sudden visual contact with a whole head knocked the wind out of me, and the spicy *panforte* I'd just eaten turned to granite in my stomach.

A head is very intimate; a person's face, like her name, is our source of recognition. Within this head had once resided the seat of reason and decision-making, the particular chemistry, the unique personality of a 14th century woman many still recognize as having been an inspiring humanitarian and Christian mystic.

For a fleeting moment I grasped the honor paid by the Catholic Church to St. Catherine in her somewhat gaudy setting. I sensed how she had been loved, sensed the earthly pathos of those who had tried to make her memory in a dark world shaded with untimely death, as lovely as possible. My heart warmed to her vulnerability, to her silent, motionless offering of herself to me in that moment. I was grateful to this young woman who by any standard went the distance for Christ in her short life. And I did not feel like an idolater for thinking so.

But in that season I wasn't used to trusting such spasms of doctrinal charity for long. Nor did I possess enough confidence in my instincts to hang onto the grace of the moment. It passed quickly, leaving me back in my comfortable nit-picking analysis, wondering how anyone could be edified by looking at some old head. Still, I felt a twinge of shame. What sacrilege and waste; that the beautiful St. Catherine – incorrupt though shriveled with time in her glass case – should be publicly exposed to the nonchalance and revulsion of ignorant tourists such as myself. Suddenly chilled, I fled the church. I look back at vignettes like the moment in San Domenico as a sort of middle school of the soul. By God's grace, I haven't fled a church in years.

The day arrived for the road trip to Wichita. With Adèle and me were my friend Candice and her daughter, Gabrielle. Our priest blessed the car with a good sprinkling of holy water, we filled the gas tank and headed east out of Colorado, where the cluttered Denver skyline soon disappeared behind the earth's curve to our back. Beyond the shoulder of the interstate lay the proverbial Heartland of America. A topography and culture of contrast opened before us.

We soon passed the requisite welcome sign into Kansas – the Sunflower State – and were immediately bombarded with road signs announcing the advancing proximity of the town of Oakley, "Home of the World's Largest Prairie Dog". I imagined a rampaging seven-foot mutant rodent with buck teeth in an iron cage, testimony to the glories of nuclear testing in the desert. It couldn't be of course, but the dog *did* reside on the road to Wichita, home of relics in an actual reliquary.

"It's probably some dumb plastic statue," Adèle remarked, a little wistfully I thought. We resisted the urge to stop, knowing we'd be sorry we'd paid good money to gaze at a shameless fraud, and be tempted to buy polyresin prairie dog bookends, to boot. Our narrow escape from interstate foolishness served as an excellent metaphor for the safety of Orthodoxy where the boundaries for veneration are clear and reasonable.

This country on the other side of the car window was once called the Sea of Grass, an ocean of undulating gray-green sod bowing low to the caprices of prairie winds, roots five feet deep in the rich Kansas loam. Gone in most places is the tallgrass of that former sea. On that clear, wind-whipped day in early March, brown expanses were poised for release from the long press of winter, and the early spring sun had already waxed sufficiently toward its equinox to coax a smudge of green from the shoulder of the highway.

In such country, the horizon is essentially unbroken. That day it drew my eye to its dark, tense line flush against the unrestrained air, the boundary between heavy earth and the enormous arc of cornflower sky. Occasionally the line was broken by a lonely farmhouse and outbuildings encircled in bare, arthritic-branched trees that clawed toward that sky, etched with crisp vapor streams and piles of lumpy, slate-bottomed cumulus clouds mounding in the east. I am so like the dark, sullen earth, perpetually poised to receive the light of God that beams on me faithfully, yet I am often without the sufficient planting of His life within me. I remain barren and unyielding to the Light's effects.

Candice's Nissan cruised at a nudge above the speed limit, yet our prosaic surroundings offered so little that resembled a reference point that we barely seemed to move. Artificial speed warps perspective. I would arrive at my destination not in weeks or months like hardier pilgrims from centuries past, but in one day's time. And I would still consider the time spent on the road an inconvenience. I fussed and rustled among the folds of a wrinkled road map, fretting over the vast distance we must drive to the town of Hayes, a full two inches east from present point. I cared nothing for Hayes of course, relegating the burg unnoticed but for a full gas tank and can of tomato juice. Wichita and its gems, further ahead on these Great Plains, was the real business at hand.

This disorienting effect of artificial speed renders most postmodern people insatiable for the next moment. We are likely to underestimate the Scriptures that measure human life in increments of morning vapor or wildflowers wilted before the sun has climbed half high. I hide my poverty of spirit behind the pace I'm allowed by culture and time in history, barreling through precious life moments only half-lived while bewailing how slowly God works in me. I wonder why He seems distant during the few minutes of attention I might give Him each day, yet rarely reprimand myself for the prayerless void that deepens.

This is a tyrannous predicament and I am a willful victim of its wiles. It is great effort for me to bend inward and receive the moment instead of the relentless press outward. But today, I would make that effort. The bow of sky and its ever-changing clouds would have to be enough to give my life a sense of purpose. Like Abraham, if I want the Promised Land I must stay in the desert and abide alone with the vision until the lessons are learned.

The Jesus Prayer is for such a frantic, fussy inner life as mine, and for such a day of blessed confinement when I could do little else than ponder the strange commodity of time. So I sat with time and the Prayer, offering the humbling, mortal petition with its odd twist of mercy, offered it without caveat or condition. With the miles came the miracle of a quiet heart, always an odd sensation when I manage to attain it, a hovering with God without pressure, without past or future. With it, the recognition that I was already on pilgrimage, a journey not made for future hours spent in Wichita but every breath along the way as well. *The Canterbury Tales* is a narrative of the road, not the destination of Becket's shrine.

It is good to consider the walking pilgrims of ancient times and the rigors they would have encountered routinely. I suspect that these rigors must have enriched their encounter with the final destination. Only a medieval pilgrim's cross-marked woolen mantle separated her from the relentless weather, to which she would be constantly exposed as she journeyed hundreds or even thousands of miles. Life could be lost at any time to the ravages of the road. In contrast, that day I wore high-tech hiking shoes and a coat made of miraculous fabric that simultaneously circulates air and repels rain. I was encased from start to finish in multiple feet of plum-colored steel complete with air bags and controlled heat, propelling me smoothly down the well-maintained interstate.

Possible sacrifice of life or limb did not enter my thinking; my subconscious has a deep-welled cultural registry that includes sophisticated police protection and speedy assistance with a broken-down car. Reared in an ordered society consumed with personal safety, comfort and individual rights, I reflexively assume such security is a blessing. But without a real cost to be counted, I wonder.

We spent the following day observing the impressive offerings of the college Adèle was considering. She perspired through hours of rigorous dance classes in company with girls poised for college graduation and entrance into professional ballet careers. The hood of her sweatshirt come down ever further around her face as the day's events culminated in a stunning student recital of Balanchine choreography. It was a highly intimidating exhibition for a 16-year-old dancer to observe. The long day among this staggering concentration of intelligence and talent became its own sort of pilgrimage for us; good pilgrimages confront us with a higher standard than our own lives demonstrate. Without a heavy and even intimidating dose of awe, there is no inspiration for change.

We arrived at St. George's well before Vespers, and located the chapel of St. Michael the Archangel deep within its interior. It is a tiny place I knew *had* to be wonderful since it was dedicated to that most powerful of angels. When I entered, I had the same impression I've gotten used to every time I enter an Orthodox temple, though it never ceases to startle me a little. It is the energy shift between the world outside and the tone of the temple itself. I feel a current of otherworldly vigor in these places, an ambiance stirred and altered when flesh and blood enter the space. In comparison to the holy peace of the icons, I recognize myself as quite a different species. That evening, I resisted the urge to stutter an apology for the intrusion.

And then I saw the reliquary, a square of oak and glass flush with the icon screen. What was wrong with me? I was as flustered as a seventh grader at the school dance. I wondered if I dared – what I wasn't sure. But I *had* to dare, for I had endured stagnant blood for nine hours in a hot car to be present for this moment.

Looking through the glass, I examined opaque plastic containers containing bits of bone or cloth. They were attached to small tags with the names of luminaries like St. Barbara, St. Anna, St. John the Baptist, St. Justin Martyr (*the* Justin Martyr), and the 20th century wonder worker, St. John Maximovitch. On it went, the footprints of giants of the Faith across the centuries dwarfed for the moment in mere bits of bone in a chapel in Kansas. The complete quiet, the absolute helplessness and exposure of these tiny relics hit me hard. It was a contrast of incongruity after the rush and talent and worldly focus of the day.

Someone has described the saints as imitating the defenseless Lamb of God by becoming like Him in vulnerability; in love that is stronger than death. Each of these saints reduced on earth to scraps of mortal substance had had a mother who once studied the face of her child bright at play.

Someone had clothed and bathed and prayed over the little one. The child's bones grew strong and the adult had emerged, and somewhere over time in the recesses of the heart, each one chose to go with Christ to the death – the death of self, of every dream and hope that might roadblock the way to authentic love, to authentic personhood. The great and obvious feats of the saints – clairvoyance, altering the weather, miraculous healings – come out of that central decision to love adamantly to the end.

The choices represented in the various lives in that reliquary matter profoundly for *my* time, *my* life. Yet not one of those mothers could have fathomed that long centuries later, a naïve pilgrim on the Great Plains of America would stand beside a box of glass and wood and spiritually feast on the sacred remains of her child.

Candice and the girls left the chapel to find seats for Great Vespers. A full, fruitful stillness filled their absence. I stared into the reliquary – I, who am insignificant and distant from such holiness. Yet I felt myself among them, enclosed and included in a moment of companionship with this cream of Christianity. I caressed the glass barrier between my hand and the relics – my relics. I own them as I do the stars, moon and air. The saints are my birthright in the same way God offers me breath.

Innocent of any irreverence it might have implied, I sat down on the solea. I felt invited to do what all the saints present with God would be about in that moment; basking in His presence. There was no pink, three-legged stool in the corner with my name in curly-cues, but the hunch that I was welcome to that fellowship, welcomed by the ones whose bones or wisps of clothing rested soundlessly beside me.

"No one here is trying to sell you anything," a wordless voice whispered. The relics simply *are*. They erect no barriers; they demand nothing by way of ego, are meek in the face of all things. This then is what it means to be saintly; a personality so sanctified that a weightless speck of his mortality drives a bittersweet thorn into the heart of an ordinary person centuries removed.

The relics that day in Wichita served as a watershed for what spilled into my life afterward. Almost immediately came a rush of confidence about the reality of the Body of Christ much larger than the struggling people huddled around me on earth. Several saints came into focus as life patrons; a paralyzed nun who healed depression with her prayers in post-revolutionary Russia; a monk who knelt for months in the Sarov forest begging God to change him; the brave women who bore myrrh to the tomb of Jesus at risk to their own lives. They poured in like long-lost friends, apparently eager to befriend the likes of me in a lavish new phase of my pilgrimage as an Orthodox Christian.

At times we are almost convinced that diseased and distorted things overcome the loveliness we want to see more of in the world. Untimely death strikes a child; wars at the office water cooler rage; leaders abuse authority; ardent prayers for healing seem to go unanswered; someone's stubborn passion resists God's grace even to death. Yet against it all, the simple relic witnesses to the world as an odd catechism of hope. In a teachable moment, a humble reliquary in the heartland of America on a chilly spring day did more for me to advance the probability of what Christ stands for, than all the gems in theology tomes I might have amassed for years, with a trifle of the effect.

CHAPTER 4: Pilgrimage Without Post Cards

For who has despised the day of small things?
Zechariah 4:10

It is a trait of human nature, the notion that a spiritual journey must be of the caliber of the adventures of Marco Polo to be of any value to the soul. We prize most highly what costs the most. Add to this the human propensity to crave the perpetual Big Word and Burning Bush, extremes and excess of all kinds, especially in matters of religion. Why else have television evangelists in sequined Liberace suits heaving wheel chairs off stages?

In this spirit of excess, I conjured up a blinding vision of myself trundling on my knees in a hair shirt from Denver to San Francisco to venerate the incorrupt relics of the Russian wonder-worker St. John Maximovitch, enshrined in a church there. The relics attract thousands of pilgrims annually who come to pray in the presence of St. John's earthly remains, returning home with a vial of blessed oil and many blessings of the heart.

When I considered the extreme sanctity of St. John and the respect his selfless life deserves, any cost to get there seemed a pittance. Especially when I compare him to shallow me, currently sulking because I haven't found just the right pair of gray winter slacks. An extended knee workout in the Salt Lake desert would do me good.

The only drawback was time. A venture like this could take months if one factored in the many deep and annoying chasms that crisscross Nevada. The distance between Denver and coastal California positively brims with daunting features you can read about on the internet: the Valley of Fire, the Loneliest Highway in America, and worst, the town of Rachel, Nevada, considered the UFO capital of the world. With my hair shirt and unusual travel mode, it would be my luck to attract the attention of bored extraterrestrials cruising the vicinity, and be abducted. I'd be dropped off at my house days later with Cheerio-shaped burn marks and a blank mind. And I'd have to start the pilgrimage all over again.

I decided to wait for more realistic conditions to visit St. John. Jerusalem, the ultimate destination of Christian pilgrimage, was also out of the question. So were St. Petersburg and the glories of the Romanian monasteries. But there would be nothing to prevent me from considering a reflective pilgrimage of meek duration and modest proportions, say, a quarter tank of gas away. God is not dependent on the sensational. In the unobtrusive and local, God and His Church are as much at work as at St. John's shrine or the Church of the Holy Sepulchre and its yearly miracle of Holy Fire.

Several from my parish had visited the Monastery of the Protection of the Holy Virgin, a women's monastic community outside the mountain hamlet of Lake George, several hours from where I live. It was close, and its name sounded deliciously, well, *holy*. The timing and scenario of this visit would be perfect. An issue from years previous had been elbowing its way to the forefront of my conscience. Now my conscience was giving me the ride of my life. It seemed like sin, yet it was a mystery to me that I hadn't been convicted about it during the many sacramental confessions I'd made in the years I'd been Orthodox.

In any case, the thing was gnawing at me now. And I was resisting it. I needed a place to order myself before God and His Church. Monasteries are intended to be sanctuaries from the distractions of the world. The daily schedule of prayer, work and worship to which monastics around the world submit themselves proves that for these people, nothing is more important than the pursuit of God. Surely in such an environment I could get the perspective I needed.

I wrestled with my calendar and made a call to the superior of the monastery, Mother Cassiana. She was friendly on the phone, and willing to receive me. On Friday afternoon, I wound up U.S. Route 24 through the gentle topography of Park County – the geographical center of Colorado east of the Continental Divide. The road quickly gained in altitude outside Colorado Springs, snaking past mountain towns of alternating dilapidation or tourist slick including a tiny enclave of mobile homes and a miniscule general store known as Bust, which boasts a population of two.

Outside the open truck window, my eyes gorged on the gentle, yielding beauty of fresh meadows at midsummer that undulated up broad knolls bordered with open-canopy ponderosa pine and stands of quaking aspen. An hour later, inside a labyrinth of dusty mountain roads, the monastery appeared at the top of a hill. It was a modest, ranch-style house set back from the road and no different at first glance from other homesteaders' homes tucked into the folds all across the surrounding mountainous ranch land. I owe my surprise at the size of the place to having lived in France, where everything – people, cars, meals – is very small *except* monasteries and historical churches, which are all huge. The *Grande Chartreuse* for instance, appears to go on for acres.

With or without the neatly lettered sign that signaled the monastery, I would have known it immediately by the small coppery roof dome. In

Orthodox architecture, this dome symbolizes the open heavens and marks the chapel's location within the monastery, its most intimate focus and spiritual center. Before I'd turned off the ignition I knew the Nicene Creed would be supported at that heart, and prayers to the Trinity lifted up day and night from this center of worship. That there are few surprises in Orthodox worship is always a stabilizing thought.

The air was spicy with the resin of fir and spruce extracted under the hot sun. A powerful stillness filled my ears after the rumble of the truck; a sense of destination waylaid my heart. Violent hail earlier in the week had thinned out the wild flowers in the airy fields around the monastery, but creamy mariposa and Indian paintbrush still dotted the meadow rises in their clear, uncomplicated beauty. I was flush with the simple happiness of presence at the edge of an adventure, freedom for the eyes and spirit everywhere I looked.

I wondered whether to wait for someone to appear, or to find a door and knock. I hated to interrupt the holy people within who might be at prayer. Was there a secret knock? Better to wait. The monastery chickens scratched in the dirt around the periphery of the house, around cords of firewood someone had recently split – ready for woodstoves in the approaching autumn days. At this altitude, snow in September would not be unusual. In the background, hummingbirds hovered around feeders hung outside a window. Except for the tiny birds, the lazy cackling of chickens and the swish of wind in the pines, there wasn't a sound.

My eye was drawn to an altar-like structure hewn of carefully fitted stones in the hollow of a field below the house, centered with a carved trefoil cross. I descended tipsy stone steps past a vast vegetable garden mangled by the hail. Below the garden was the monastery cemetery. Allotted the holy duty of receiving the dead, the soft, grassy plot lay innocent in the sunshine, unmarked as yet by gravestones.

Then my throat caught to notice a cross marking one tiny grave apart, ringed with white stones; the child of a local priest. A pulsation of dormant grief surged across my heart at the sight of the baby's grave. It was the muffled memory of my own lost baby, unborn so long ago. Worn by time, the old sorrow resurfaces in cycles, often signaling that some apparently unrelated expression within me is poised for emergence. With the renegade grief that morning was the hope that in that still, still place apart from everyday concerns, I'd feel the flutter of a few heartbeats from my inner life; the life that is so often stifled by the press of schedule and the noise of daily concerns. If old grief could lay some of that bare, I welcomed it.

This was why I'd come after all, to move out of the superficial flow, to drift in a quiet eddy of spiritual retreat; a rearrangement in my awareness of the familiar.

A small woman in the habit of the Russian Orthodox nun appeared around the corner of the house, accompanied by a medium sized, reddish dog. Koper is the official monastery dog, distinguished to my mind by the fact that I didn't hear him bark once during my stay. His conduct seemed well suited to a place dedicated to peace and quiet.

Mother Cassiana led the way across a sunny deck and into the main house. Icons on a small entry table stood immediate sentinel to one of the benchmarks of the monastery: Saints Watching Over All. Beyond the entryway was an open kitchen with a long wooden table and benches. The kitchen was a paragon of comfortable American mainstream. Refrigerator magnets clutched photos of the sisters' friends and families, a flowered porcelain teapot perched atop a bread box. Sunshine and peppery mountain air poured through the open window along with the industrious vibrations of the hummingbirds.

In the adjoining room were the couches and coffee tables found in anyone's living room. Potted plants soaked up the mountain sun, a laptop computer sat open on a table. It occurred to me that this was also a home. Those who cloak themselves in black and vow to pray for the world are like anyone else in their need to occasionally sit down somewhere or use a word processor. I thought of the innocuous rural field in Christ's parable of the hidden treasure. The jewel waiting to be unearthed lies beneath the prosaic, the daily.

Amidst the icons dotting the walls of the living area were framed photos of two people who've had significant influence in Mother Cassiana's life during the extended sojourns she has spent in the Romanian monastery of Varatec. One was a half profile of a smooth-skinned 78 year-old nun, Mother Onufria. The face was serene, on her mouth the hint of a self-effacing smile. Mother Onufria's life could not be more antithetical to the American lifestyle norm. She entered the convent of Varatec at the age of 12, in an era when Romanian law permitted this. Despite her limited formal education in the world, she knows English, French and German. She serves at Varatec as guide to non-Romanian visitors. Mother Cassiana describes her as an exquisite model of humility and innocence.

Mounted nearby was a photo of the 20th century Elder Cleopa, a clairvoyant spiritual elder of the Romanian people whom Mother Cassiana knew when he was alive and whose biography the monastery has translated and published in English. On the elder's face was the expression of many people like him; a paradox of submission and resistance. This elder would no doubt have been one to sell everything in order to spend his life digging among the weeds and rock in the ordinary field of the parable until he found the hidden treasure. I felt left behind in my own awkward hacking at the rough ground, where it would seem I am constantly misplacing the shovel.

It was time for tea, poured from the flowered teapot at the big kitchen table. Mother Cassiana had agreed beforehand to talk with me, though she had stipulated beforehand that monastics prefer not to be asked too many personal questions. Their focus is, after all, to pray and manage the monastery, not satisfy the too-curious visitor. But in the United States, monasticism is still an unusual choice, and people can't help but be curious as to why someone might choose this path. It's one thing to read about 4th century Egyptian folk who embraced living in caves in the desert as a backdrop for their salvation. It's something else to sip tea with a contemporary human being who returns calls from an answering machine and takes her car for an oil change.

Mother Cassiana explained that as a teenager she was haunted by an urgent inner question: *"And then what?"* She recalls being acutely aware of the transience of the present life. She was unimpressed with the vain offerings of postmodern American culture. She attended church and began to observe life through the lens of the Gospel, increasingly uncomfortable with what she felt was a dysfunctional backdrop of cultural norms in which people – herself included – were expected to live out their lives. She noticed that even in the Church, young people were strongly encouraged to get as much education as possible, in order to acquire a good job and the accoutrements of a comfortable life for themselves and a family. Spiritual acquisition seemed to take a back seat.

"*And then what?*" she continued to ask herself, dreading being a casualty to a system that might limit her capacity to serve God. The teenager became adamant that her life would count for the radical things Christ preached, no matter how awkwardly set against the status quo they might appear.

After high school graduation, she visited the Monastery of the Transfiguration in Ellwood, Pennsylvania. There she discovered a context in which a life of spiritual fullness seemed possible. A few days among the nuns, the services and deep attention to prayer was all it took to clinch her decision. "With me, it couldn't be halfway. It had to be all or nothing." She entered the monastery permanently a few months later.

"When God calls you to the monastic life, He offers His grace. If you don't respond promptly, He withdraws that grace. Women have told me over the years they sense they are being called to this, yet want to finish college, travel or experience 'life' before they come. They get distracted, meet a nice man, never come back. I've watched some people try to recreate the joy and grace they had when God called them. Because they should have embraced monasticism and settled for something else, they admit they aren't really at peace."

She believes there is tremendous protection in the monastic choice. During her long stays at Varatec, she observed an unusual innocence among the sisters who had entered monasteries as children. As in the case of Mother Onufria, separation from the world at a young age enables these people to retain much of their childlike purity of heart, the possession of which the Scriptures claim enables one to see God.

There was much to think about. The tea things were put away and the nuns and a few pilgrims stepped through the side door of the kitchen into the monastery chapel. There we were enveloped in the inexplicable peace of Vespers. Wooed by icons, drawn in by incense, it is in the midst of one of these services – any of them – that I am always reminded of why I embraced Eastern Orthodoxy in the first place; balance, dignity… rightness. Gone is the twinge I often had in my former tradition, that the people who had organized the service were running as scared as I was.

I said Vespers that evening not only with those present in that local monastery, but with the Orthodox Church across the world as well. Lampadas flickered, incense increased in pungency, leading body and soul deeper into prayer. Tiny waves of the goodness of worship lapped at my spirit, coaxing me toward noble thoughts and feelings, toward the Trinity and the saints.

Summer twilight was dusting the air blue outside the chapel window when Vespers ended. We made parting venerations to Christ and the saints, and stepped back through the chapel door into the homey kitchen for supper. Soon we separated for private prayer and sleep in the deepening evening.

As though distilled to greater concentration by the counterpoint potency of Vespers, the annoying issue that had been working its way upward inside me had now increased in intensity. In the guest quarters, I pulled shades against the mountain night, inky and star-stabbed. How anemic is city darkness compared to this. The night pressed in, and with it the loneliness that keeps company with a troubled conscience. The nightlight from the bathroom cast a weak sheen on the icons arranged on a high shelf opposite the bed. My eye on the haloed ones, I finally descended into sleep.

Saturday morning I stumbled outside to an eastern sky washed in apricot, tying on a head covering for the first time in my church life. I had been advised that monasteries prefer women wear a scarf or small shawl on the head during services, after the admonishment of St. Paul that women cover their heads in prayer. I have no convictions one way or the other about headgear in church, and know only a few women who practice this custom, so I was content to honor the context of the monastery in this way.

As Matins progressed I discovered I liked the feel of the scarf around my face. Like a prayer rope in my hand when I walk in our neighborhood's open space, it reminded me more keenly of what we were about in church, as though God rested His hand lightly on my head. I wondered if such a habit could retain this reminding quality, or whether its impact would fade with familiarity. Knowing me, I'd lose the scarf somewhere and that would be the end of it.

> To the Theotokos let us run now most earnestly, we sinners all and wretched ones, and fall down, in repentance calling from the depths of our souls: O Lady, come unto our aid, have compassion upon us; hasten thou, for we are lost in a throng of transgressions. Turn not thy servants away with empty hands, for thee alone do we have as our only hope.

Through the poetic language of the Theotokion of Matins that morning I became more aware of something that had been on the periphery of my consciousness the previous evening during Vespers. I would feel the full impact of this phenomenon again during the Saturday Vigil. While I heard my voice pour out the Theotokion's rich, honest emotion, I became aware that someone else was present besides the human beings in the room, ephemeral yet very real. It was as though a tender prompter stood at my elbow, nourishing the readings with her presence, rounding out the words herself as I spoke them. I took this synergy with my unseen helper completely for granted at the time. It seemed expected in the heightened spiritual atmosphere.

When Matins was over I walked back through the chapel door into the kitchen where the dreamlike reality of the past hours made contact with a normal summer morning on earth. Two steps into the kitchen I stopped. A little bell was ringing softly in my mind. I stood completely still as a realization washed through me: *Mary the Mother of God is the patron saint of this monastery.* And then I knew. It had been *her*, Christ's mother, wedged in the chapel with us since the first rays of sun.

I stifled the urge to claw at my hair. What's a sinner to *do* when the top Saint of the Church joins the choir for Matins? I looked around, waiting for harp music, expecting to see angels perched on rainbows around the room. But all was familiar and orderly. Orange toaster coils browned fresh-baked bread, hummingbirds hovered around their feeders while visitors chatted quietly over mugs of tea. Immediately, the amazing occurrence of only minutes ago became like a cloud in the summer sky that changes shape before one can decide exactly what it looks like. How elusive is the interface between the temporal world of our senses and the one that thrives outside three dimensions, beyond eyes that see so little. What I'd experienced was too foreign, the muscles of my spirit too flabby to sustain the contraction for long. Thoughts of a hot breakfast were more real. What was familiar drew me back in, while the other faded to words in my journal.

Mother clattered pans in the big sunny kitchen, an honest activity as much a part of the rhythm of monastic life as prayers. Because of the extended time they spend at prayer, many monastics are probably accustomed to the felt presence of the saints. The bulk of their vocation's energy is bent toward daily pushing the entreaties of the Church against walls of spiritual darkness, invoking God and the intercession of myriad holy ones as they go.

I was surprised after breakfast when Mother suggested a walk with Koper in the national forest. I knew there had to be numerous projects begging for her attention. I changed out of my long skirt into jeans, and slathered plenty of sunscreen against the high altitude sun. Koper wagged his tail in eagerness for the outing, loaded with his own water in the doggy backpack. He trotted happily at Mother's side, the picture of canine contentment.

Wind rustled high in the ponderosa pines as we traversed meadows and picked up a trail through the trees. A watery tang in the air suggested rain. An early afternoon bank of clouds had scuttled our way off the mountain range to the west in the predictable weather pattern of the Colorado high country. In the distance, high on the Continental Divide, the local Orthodox come together each January on the Feast of the Epiphany for the Blessing of the Waters of our nation on both sides of the Divide.

I continued to be perplexed by the issue that ate away at my peace. It felt as thick and heavy as a callous. Yet I felt a slight breaking up of its fibers; the richness of Matins had done its progressive work of peeling back layers of denial. Still, my mind resisted: *Maybe it hadn't been sin, just my hypersensitive conscience kicking up dust in midlife. Why hadn't I felt this bad about it years ago?*

The late priest and theologian Alexander Schmemann wrote in his journals that he rarely heard an actual confession. Instead, he was obliged to listen almost exclusively to sly litanies of blame, in which the antagonist in the story he was hearing played the role of slug, thug or litterbug responsible for the would-be penitent's predicament. Fr. Schmemann would not be the first priest, psychologist, parent or police officer to marvel at human mastery of the defense mechanism of projection. In my own soul's quandary, I could easily blame the other people involved. But it was I after all who was miserable. It was I who needed humility. "A penitent is a buyer of humility," wrote St. John Climacus.

Walking next to me that afternoon of scuttling clouds was one whose every breath had been officially consecrated to the pursuit of God. I'd have been a fool not to drag her and her silent dog into the drama at hand. Her advice was sound; confession was imperative. Satan is usually vague in his accusations. God is crystal clear, squeezing hard on the specifics. I was drowning in specifics. Pride relaxed its grip.

We circled back toward the monastery, faces to the wind that had whipped a slight chill into the warm air and cleared my head. I was eager to return to the chapel, to find myself again amidst the saints, candles, incense and semi-darkness. I knew the monastery was serving powerfully as a catalyst for my remorse, as well as a bookmark for prayers I'd left off earlier in the day; I consider this resource one of the Church's gateways to the transcendent. And I knew the chapel's pull on my spirit was also about the presence of that mysterious Mother of God who had joined us earlier. No cluster of candles, no "religious art" had the power to draw a soul back in such a way.

In the darkness of this present world, infested with the spirits of ancient lies, it is a miracle that anyone for any reason desires God. It is a miracle anyone acknowledges Him as First Cause or reaches to hold Him in the darkness or sings His praise on a mountaintop. It is a miracle that I, a fallen daughter of Eve, would find myself eager to confess my view of reality in the Sacrament of Repentance.

It was time for the Saturday night prayer vigil. "Vigil" sounded daunting, like something that could last all night if we weren't careful. Medieval pilgrims who kept vigil at the shrine of St. Thomas Becket would lean against chilly pillars through the night until dawn, often in bare feet on that cold stone. I'd read about the vigils of the early centuries of the Church, when Saturday night services started near sunset with a two-hour Vespers. Afterward, people were given a snack of wine and blessed bread while they listened to someone read the entire book of Acts. Next came Matins, a good three hours. Finally, the First Hour prayers were read, wrapping up the 8-hour ordeal around 4 o'clock in the morning. This gave worshippers a few hours to nap before returning to church for the Sunday morning Divine Liturgy, the spiritual high point of the week that would last another three to four hours.

Mother had not hinted at anything like a venture of this magnitude, but I entered the chapel with my running shoes laced up tight. The length and density of readings looked overwhelming to me; the service books are inches thick. Yet this is the office entrusted daily to monastic communities around the world. I am convinced that the constancy and fervency of such large-scale prayer contributes heavily to the miraculous fact that this tumultuous planet still endures.

We moved through the prescribed order; where one hymn, chant or reading ended and the next began, I wouldn't know. All was a seamless ribbon threading one prayer to the next, as afternoon went down to the golden end of day, squeezing itself through squares of the chapel windows, mixing creation with human language to herald the arrival of another Lord's Day, born each Sabbath sunset.

I was to do the Kathisma readings, potent selections from the Psalms alternated with other texts read by the nuns. Their understanding of liturgics is fine-tuned, and they moved expertly back and forth between the big liturgical volumes on the chanters' stand.

Nowhere else in Scripture is the soul and its gamut of emotions laid so bare as in the Psalms. David's helplessness, his personal wretchedness is immortalized for the human race in these plaintive entreaties to God: *bring my soul out of prison*. Incrementally, the readings were dissolving the last tissues of callous, melting my will before God's, that His be done. I wobbled at the chanters' stand, shaking the bars. Through a choked voice, the relentless Kathisma dug and exposed until a cathartic pool brimmed to tears and I found myself on a chair, working through a box of tissues while someone else picked up the thread of readings.

Later I huddled with a phone card on the cool tile floor in front of the monastery bookstore. In his uncanny, nonjudgmental way, my confessor turned the evening of my contrition into an encounter quite without humiliation to me, in every way movement forward into life. The Sacrament is meant to heal.

When I resurfaced, the house was heavy with the drowsy calm of bedtime. I let myself out of the building for the short walk to the guest quarters. Far from city lights, the immense, tree-rimmed sky hung low with its weight of stars. I lifted my face to the glittering firmament, overcome with that age-old awe about infinity and the mystery of human purpose that gazing at the night sky seems to bring out of people.

Life is "a few handbreadths" in length, yet when taking in the stars, most human hearts throb with the assurance that the soul contains eternity, an "entire universe" as one saint explains it. St. Macarius wrote that the "heart is but a small vessel; and yet dragons and lions are there. There likewise is God, there are the angels, the heavenly cities and the treasures of grace; all things are there."

Nothing exists in a vacuum. The direction each heart takes matters. Confession of sin matters. To acknowledge even a seemingly small thing that has distorted the order of the universe has a healing effect on that entire order on some level. Like ripples in a pond, a gentle movement of goodness radiates outward from a central conviction.

I turned my eyes from the fathomless sky and pulled the shutters one last time, curling into the soft protection of bed to face the icons.

CHAPTER 5: At Least Consider the Lilies – Diary of a Silent Retreat

Silence is God's first language.
St. John of the Cross

On the Day of Arrival:

So I've done the deed, paid good money and checked in for a six-day silent retreat high on a mesa the color of straw. The grounds of the Sacred Heart Jesuit Retreat House are dotted with chapels, a lily pond and eyeless white statues of saints; St. Jude, St. Joseph and the tallest statue of the Virgin Mary I've ever seen. This afternoon I put myself in the car with a gym bag, a pair of running shoes and a wide-brimmed hat and drove an hour into the foothills south of Denver. I had convinced myself at the time that I would be better for a few days of silence. But barely. The more I learn about what a silent retreat entails, the more intimidated I am.

The four Jesuit priests who run this place aren't messing around. It's been made clear that except for a short optional appointment each day with a spiritual director who is assigned to help each retreat-goer process his or her experiences throughout the week, the 40-odd people gathered here will not speak a single word. There will be no stimulating speaker every morning upon whose pearls we might ruminate all afternoon. No small groups, ice breakers, workshops or coffee breaks. Outside of silent mealtimes, optional daily Mass and time with the spiritual director, there is no agenda.

As I understand it, we are to pass each other in the halls and shower rooms and on the vast grounds in abstention from spoken interaction of all kinds; casual banter, heart-felt dialogue, rousing arguments, singing in the shower, and all attempts to entertain, comfort or exhort anyone on any topic for any reason whatsoever, amen. So far, no one has mentioned "Grand Silence", an optional feature of this type of retreat that even forbids eye contact with others. Lord have mercy, if I'm not allowed even to *look* at people for the next week.

Though most of the present group will stay for eight long days, I've elected with a few others for the six-day Spiritual Midget option. I'll miss the final morning when the eight-day group gathers for their reward – a *talking* breakfast. As satisfying as that would be, it has to be factored into the equation that I am a hopeless extrovert. Whatever there might be to prove or to glean, six days will have to be sufficient.

In the parking lot when I arrived, a portly man whistled cheerfully as he bolted a mountain bike to the back of his Honda. He had just finished his own retreat a few hours earlier, and offered to help me find my room. I asked him to tell me more about this mysterious experience before me – the silent retreat.

"Oh, I've done about eleven of these," he answered vaguely as he led the way up a narrow flight of stairs, whistling all the while. He seemed to possess that uncomplicated enjoyment of his own existence I always admire, yet find so elusive for myself. He opened the door to my room, heaved in my luggage and left me to myself.

The east-facing room I'll occupy for the next six days cannot be locked from the outside, nor will they lock the main doors of the building at night. Though I don't know what the point of that is, we are consequently at each other's mercy here, and at the mercy of local renegades and axe murderers. The room overlooks a spacious lawn stretching across the breadth of the mesa, dropping down to meadows and scrub-covered hills. The lawn is bleached gold in the relentless heat of this summer of ungenerous clouds. The leaves of numerous shade trees shudder slightly in currents created by the hot, oppressive air.

I forgot to pack toothpaste. And my hymnbook and sleep mask. But out of the abundance of the suitcase priorities speak; thankfully I've brought along enough earrings to accessorize ten women for a month. I never unpack when I travel so there was little to do but kick the suitcase under the bed and arrange a few icons on the small dresser.

The tiny room is very clean, and apart from a crucifix over the bed and a laminated sign detailing bed linen protocol, it is devoid of decoration. It smells vaguely of vanilla and fabric softener. The room keeps an impersonal distance from me as I sit on the bed, as though protecting itself from attachment to me; just one of an endless stream of silent pilgrims that have come and gone over the years. I feel a little like Dante in the gloomy wood before his descent into hell, gone from the path direct.

To shake off the gloomy wood sensation, I found an exit through the dining room downstairs and walked the periphery of the property, pondering the subject of retreat, theoretically the reason I'm here. The word triggers memories of church youth group excursions; woodsy, adrenal-depleting weekends of gorging on Kum-ba-ya, ghost stories and best of all, giggling forays to the boys' bathroom late at night for the grand adventure of stretching saran wrap across the toilet seats. I suppose God was around someplace.

By college, the miracle of maturation had rendered my friends and me experts on God. We were decisive about Him and His ways with a confidence that takes my breath away now. Our convictions were reflected in many late-night prayer sessions heavy with vows to live for things absolute and unambiguous, things we'd die for at the stake if need be.

All grown up now, I can't remember the last time I retreated. Life seems to have been stuck on fast-forward for many years. The website for Sacred Heart described their center as "a place from which to see clearly." The outward view from these heights is inspiring, sweeping in every direction across rolling hills and further west to peaks that climb into the dome of the Colorado sky. But it is the clearer view within themselves that pilgrims come here to hone. Without social interaction, televisions or computers, we will be faced with ourselves without distraction.

As a guide to this clearer inner view, participants at Sacred Heart are encouraged to explore the *Spiritual Exercises* of St. Ignatius Loyola, medieval founder of the Society of Jesus. The *Exercises* are a series of meditations, prayers and mental exercises, which have as their objective to fit a person to be a companion of Jesus.

St. Ignatius designed his program to be practiced during retreats of precisely thirty days. Silence was considered imperative to hear the voice of God, to explore the movement of the heart. In recent times many Catholic retreat centers have modified the program to accommodate the reality of modern life; hence the innovation of six or eight days.

As helpful as I'm sure they are, I've decided to forego St. Ignatius and his *Exercises*. I skimmed some of them; the vocabulary, phrasing and mind-set are, understandably, very Roman Catholic, such as these instructions from the Exercises of the first week on examining conscience: "Let him make in the first line of the G---- as many dots as were the times he has fallen into that particular sin or defect."

As a Protestant-turned-Orthodox, this kind of counting is too foreign. Traditionally, Catholics were trained from their earliest stints in the confessional to recount the number of times a sin was committed; it is part of their spiritual work. But I can't make up for lost time in a week. Besides, I don't know what a "G----" is.

I can probably achieve some of what St. Ignatius had in mind through a good re-reading of St. Theophan's *The Spiritual Life and How to Be Attuned to It: A Study in the Science of the Soul.* In this book, a 19th century Russian monk offers down-to-earth spiritual advice to a young woman probably still in her teens whom God was leading gradually into the monastic vocation.

In any case, the common denominator for all participants here – whatever they choose to do with their time – is strict silence. When I ran the idea past my own spiritual director, Fr. Mark was hesitant. He was probably suppressing incredulous laughter at the notion of *me* being quiet for a single day – let alone six – and because he was about to explain that this type of exercise is not part of the normal Orthodox model for developing one's faith.

"When we Orthodox go on retreat, we retreat in community, for we are saved in community." This comment surprised me, in light of the number of recluses and hesychasts with which our Orthodox history is replete; men and women solitaries who spent months and even years in seclusion to cultivate their relationship with God.

That's different, Fr. Mark explained. The majority of these people were already well-advanced in their spirituality after years of struggle and obedience to an advisor, usually monastics that had gone into silence gradually and under direction. To be abruptly immersed in a week of complete silence seemed to him like dabbling with pseudo-spirituality, as though someone took an idea – solitude in this case – and built an artificial structure around it. Without the larger context of the Church to buffer such an undertaking, a silent retreat for its own sake might be too forced, even harmful.

Ultimately he suggested I try it, just for the experience. But he cautioned me about too much inward-looking, and reminded me to bring hand puppets, since eventually I'd be compelled to communicate with someone, somehow.

It's later now, and I'm back in my room after a gathering downstairs for formal introductions. Most of these people are Roman Catholics; laity, priests, and nuns of orders that no longer wear the habit. There are also several local Protestant pastors who to a man look desperately in need of rest. The balance is a mix of people from many walks of life; students, therapists, professors, dreamy-looking souls, and me. Most interesting is a small contingency of 20-somethings who have been here almost thirty days already on the silence track. St. Ignatius fans, no doubt.

After introductions, Mass was celebrated. I did not receive Communion, nor will I this week, since Orthodox beliefs do not coincide with Catholic ones. I tried not to look prissy and exclusivist as I sat still with my hands folded. As the others approached the chalice, including the Protestant pastors, I felt the pang of exclusion from something vital, longed-for. Conflicting doctrines aside, I'm still hungry for the Eucharist.

After Mass, the Jesuits and the two lay counselors who round out the staff of six hosted a short punch-and-cookie time in the main lounge. This was our one chance to "get to know" our fellow retreat-goers before the ban of silence would come crashing down. I felt like the proverbial deer in the headlights, knowing it to be impossible in the space of half an hour to blather enough words to enough people sipping punch in a room badly in need of air conditioning to convince them of how pretty, witty and wise I am. So I opted to stand in a corner like a lump.

Others were giving the assignment a valiant go, and I had to appreciate the strain of the exercise. The scene reminded me of the old T.V. game show in which winning contestants were turned loose in a grocery store with shopping carts and given something like ten minutes to load the carts with whatever they wanted from the shelves. It was morbidly fascinating to watch otherwise respectable Betty Crocker housewives grunt with exertion at the meat counter as they heaved massive armloads of pork roasts into their carts. The cruel fact is that there just isn't enough time to shop in this manner without losing some of one's dignity forever.

Without time to do justice to the event, I too would only have made a fool of myself. I would have worked the lounge on fast forward to find out, for instance, if the melancholy-intellectual type over there actually does stand-up comedy on the side like I suspect – the snag there being no future opportunity to redeem myself if I insulted him with the question. Or I might have offended the sweet little nuns in street clothes, plying them with ungracious questions about how they *really* feel about the veil they left behind them and snorting out rude opinions on Vatican II and that sort of thing.

So I turned my attention to the books on the library shelf behind me, feigning indifference to the chatter around me. They're big on the Twelve Steps and other addiction recovery methods here. I wonder about the value of silent retreat for someone in addiction recovery. I'd be tempted to feel doubly deprived, not being allowed to talk *or* ingest Jack Daniels. It's probably a mixed bag. According to St. Kosmos Aitolos, "Stillness helps us by making evil inoperative; it is the most direct support in attaining dispassion."

On the other hand, St. John Climacus warned, "He who is sick in soul from some passion and attempts stillness is like a man who has jumped from a ship into the sea and thinks that he will reach the shore safely on a plank."

But back to me. Standing there with my empty punch cup I suddenly felt very silly and self-indulgent to be away while our yard at home was in dire need of weeding. Not to mention my panic at forfeiting my right to exercise the precious vocal chords that have blessed so many for so many years. I fought down the impulse to gather everyone 'round and recite Emily's graveyard soliloquy from *Our Town*, just to show those folks I know a thing or two. This felt like the night before the vegan fast of Great Lent starts every spring and I am tempted to eat a washtub of pot roast, because I still *can*. And I wonder; if I make this sacrifice, will there be anything left of me?

Day One

I woke to a dawn of birds, the fresh scent of early day and… silence. This was reasonable considering the hour; there was no need for alarm. I watched an orange morsel of sun nibble its way upward between an elm tree and the chapel steeple outside my window. At that window facing the sunrise, I prayed the morning prayers of the Church. Then I was anxious to explore the several hundred acres of hiking paths that make up most of the land that belongs to the center.

I let myself out of the main grounds through a rickety gate in the barbed wire fence. The gate opened onto a path heavily traveled by cows, judging from the profusion of their pies. In this trail-runner's paradise I spent a good hour dodging cow pies among the scrub oak and sage, thinking hard about silence and making hilarious comments to myself to which I responded with hearty laughter. When I returned, the house was as ghostly still as when I'd left.

Except that now it was unnatural silence, because people were up and around – lots of them. The ghostly stillness was coming *directly from them*. These wraiths slithered into shower rooms and bathed soundlessly under the hiss of steamy cascades. They ducked behind corners on slippers of air, profoundly avoided my eyes and smiled sweetly at someone just past my left ear – God I suppose. My brochure tells me they're supposed to be acting like this, but I'm already softly stamping my little foot. How addicted I am to people – one of the frivolous pleasantries of life!

I entered the dining room for breakfast to the most awkward social setting I've ever encountered. It was worse than a funeral. I knew these must be sincere, respectable people by the looks of their clean kakis and the number of Bibles they were carrying. But here it ended, and I hardly knew what to make of the tableau before me, reminiscent of a zombie movie where aliens have sucked the souls out of peoples' bodies, leaving only Stepford wives behind.

With much gliding and serenity my fellow retreat-goers gathered toast at the buffet, then dreamily took their places at tables for six where they proceeded to ignore everyone completely. Instead, there was much grave staring into coffee, or into thick, important-looking books. Or more frightening yet, out into the Great

Beyond, a place that must open itself exclusively to those who do silent retreats every summer.

Tasteful cello music wafted over the intercom as people shook pink packets into their coffee. They even managed to retrieve the saltshaker from the other end of the table without moving a muscle. It must go with the territory, the ability to bend matter with the mind or exploit the possibilities of the fourth dimension. I couldn't shake the impression that I'd burst in on a lair of Gnostics.

Reluctantly I joined the line. The tasteful cello music began to whine, as is often the wont of cello music. "Contemplate something, you peasant," it droned as I collected silverware and a tray. "Relish this splendid silence, whip up some quotable quotes, and pay attention to that sorry excuse for an interior life of yours." Then came the mocking thought that cultivating my sorry excuse for an interior life might not be possible, might come at a price too high to pay, especially without St. Ignatius.

I felt worn out before I'd quite decided between ham and bacon at the steam table. I couldn't face the ignoring at the tables for six, so I took my tray into the garden area outside the dining room. This is where I now sit, at a table for two without the two, in the shade of an enormous cottonwood facing a tangle of rose bushes and day lilies and a stone sundial. *Tempus Fugit* is carved into the rim – *Time Flees*. Four or five other people also sit in lonely breakfast vigil at other tables for two, chewing and staring south toward the large marble Stations of the Cross. I hear birds, the hum of a fan from the kitchen. But there's no sound from my fellows here in the garden, with whom – somehow – I'm on retreat.

Later: I've just finished lunch, and even though I prayed and read the Bible and St. Theophan all morning with my chin cupped contemplatively in my hand, I still have a rotten attitude about everyone eating alone together. The silence also accentuates my life-long annoyance with *the sight of people eating at all.* Especially like this, sitting up straight and proper with their hands folded politely in their laps. But there is no one to be polite *for.*

Couldn't God have just skipped this aspect of the human condition, this humiliating, pathetic drive to take time out from more worthwhile pursuits to place pieces of plants and animals into holes in our faces and then *swallow* all that stuff? At least He could have arranged for us to eat standing up, as seen everywhere at posh sushi bars, or hot dog kiosks on the sidewalks of Manhattan. People on the sidewalks of Manhattan never look pathetic as they eat. Wearing something in gray (the new black), they are on the cusp of an exciting job interview for which they'll actually be hired. For these off-hand standers-up, eating is only a casual pause in their hip, high-purpose day, never a humiliating spectacle.

This is where talking comes in. Talking while eating diffuses the lowliness factor. We're relaxed and distracted while talking, making us appear less prehistoric than we really are. A stimulating discussion on the imminent demise of whoever keeps hogging all the cool cereal around the house averts our attention from the sight of each other masticating things.

Afternoon: I had an appointment with the spiritual director. It was a short one. What were my goals, my plans for the silent retreat, she wanted to know. Her eyes sparkled. Wow, she *loves* this stuff. She looked disappointed when I told her I'd come here mostly out of curiosity, but perked up slightly when I suggested that a silent retreat might be a type of pilgrimage. Yes, definitely a subset of pilgrimage, she glowed. She seemed to be suppressing the desire to paste a gold star on my shirt. I doubt I'll have many of these meetings.

I took a hot, restless nap in a hammock on the lawn facing the mountains. I woke up disoriented and hungry, to the sound of lonely wind sifting in the tree overhead. I'd hit a wall while I slept. The absolute reality of imposed silence and social isolation settled in, dark and heavy. It wasn't as though I'd been craving solitude when I arrived, like some of these poor souls probably had.

I've had a quiet summer so far; sewing, watching my teenagers roll their eyes, consolidating partial sticks of butter onto one dish, fighting my little battles with bindweed among the hollyhocks. I don't need to rest up or "get away" from anything, much less bask in the brilliance of my own company. But it must be borne for many a day more. According to Bishop Kallistos Ware, one of the requirements for true pilgrimage is the willingness to find oneself in a position of weakness and vulnerability. Only then, starved out of complacency, will a person seek.

Before sleep: I sat in a swinging chair on the west lawn and stared into a lingering crimson sunset. It's unnatural, this idea of sitting in swinging chairs at the end of the day without the company of a single soul with whom to share this glorious drama of light. Bishop Ware would be thrilled. I'm definitely vulnerable, without the padding of even my own voice to complete the picture I present to others. A voiceless specter in the halls, the lounge, the dining room, I must bare myself in silence, and trust that this dim sketch of self will be enough. But then I remember: no one is here to know or care anything about me.

Day Two

It's the 4th of July. Tim and I have never been apart on a major holiday. He and the kids will grill something tonight and hang over the fence to take in the Andersons' fireworks, people for whom a Roman candle is soul food. And what will I do all day? There's breakfast of course. Thank God for mealtime, despite the cloying manners and silence. Mealtimes provide some shape to the strange quality time takes on here. Bustling around the toaster, plying grape jelly to toast, pouring a second cup of coffee; all become lifesaving pastimes. They give a confused silent retreat-goer something to believe in.

I slouch with as much nonchalance as possible at my table in the garden, facing the roses and lilies and chewing without zeal so as not to remind anyone of a 1950's health textbook illustration, where two children sit up straight in their chairs wearing side parts and Peter Pan collars, obediently chewing their four food groups while Mother in helmet hair looks on approvingly. And another thing: why am I the only one who makes any noise while cracking the shells on these hard boiled eggs they serve every morning?

I hear the weak peeping of birds and look up to see a robin's nest atop a stone pillar under the dining room eaves. Here a mother robin broods over four feisty young ones, mostly grown. I only assume she is the mother bird because she's working so hard to keep her ornery teenagers down in the nest where it's safe, something I identify strongly with.

Now the robin flutters away from the nest and returns with some sort of writhing wormy thing in her beak. She deposits pieces of it into a couple of the comical gaping mouths. Dad arrives with a grub, while Mom flutters away for more groceries. They follow this pattern for a good half hour.

It occurs to me that I've been mesmerized by birds and flowers for quite a while, and that everyone else has left the garden without my notice. Wonder of wonders; I've been considering the lilies of the field and the birds of the air, and how they neither toil nor spin. Not once have I jumped up to match socks or dust something. For whatever else this retreat lacks, it's giving me the luxury of reams and streams of lazy, timeless time.

Later: There was cake with red and blue icing at lunch in honor of the day, and all the chocolate ice cream you wanted. I haven't eaten chocolate ice cream since I was in grade school, when Daddy routinely brought it home in perspiring, mushy cartons after school orchestra concerts. I ate two bowls in honor of my wholesome, normal childhood. The afternoon is very hot. My comrades-at-silence glide across the scorched lawns with their Bibles and spiritual books. Heat waves distort the Stations of the Cross and bleach the sky watercolor pale.

I'm reading from Thomas Merton's *Thoughts in Solitude*, a book that some equally puzzled former guest probably once read and left behind in a heroic attempt to understand what might be gleaned from protracted silence amongst a throng.

Father Merton writes that both pride and humility seek interior silence, pride by its desire to imitate the silence of God – a desire that leads to self-ruin. Humility views silence as a reflection of one's spiritual poverty and helplessness before God. It is not speaking that breaks silence, maintains Father Merton, but the anxiety to be heard.

Alas, I *do* feel anxious to be heard, and also to hear.

End of Day: I lapped the property with my prayer rope, praying the Our Father and an amusing verse from Psalms about God setting a door of enclosure 'round about my lips. The Lord's Prayer has endless possibilities, every word a world of application. It's perfect in a setting like this, where the mind is available to almost anything that can catch its fancy. *Our* Father, *Thy* will...

I stood before the tall, white statue of the Mother of God on the south lawn, and prayed the "Akathist to the Mother of God: Nurturer of Children". No one here would think it odd to stand talking to a 15-foot statue, yet I felt exposed, unable to connect with the white, unfocused eyes. For me, religious statuary lacks the presence of the prototype I feel in icons. There is a small icon of the Vladimir Mother of God in the dining room. Its familiarity is comforting.

I curled up on a swinging bench in the dregs of another sunset, overlooking the plain below. Local families in pickup trucks and vans were congregating just across the ravine. Adults laughed and called to their friends, children squealed with excitement in anticipation of this yearly novelty of fireworks. Beer and pop cans opened with a hiss, everyone piled into the truck beds for a better view of the scintillating explosions that splattered the velvety arc above.

Homesickness and longing for belonging engulfed me as the display of lights flashed and faded. I ached at random for Mom, dead over two years, for my kids, for everyone I love; all who love *me*. My insides felt splintery, rigid, and my spine ached. I think my body is rebelling against the deprivation of joy that people bring me.

Day Three

"Even Solomon in all his glory was not arrayed like one of these."

I'm *silently* cracking the shell of my egg at breakfast, and considering the lilies again. Simple flowers of the field are superior to Solomon's attire because unlike a king's audacious robes, flowers do not incite envy; their beauty does not arouse comparison or critique. The lilies' loveliness is an artless, wide-eyed display of the glory of God. There is no Gucci bag or Rolex in the plant kingdom, nor in the Kingdom of Heaven.

Lunchtime, again: I had set my backpack on one of the garden tables before going through the lunch line. When I returned, someone was sitting there. At *my* table you see, though other tables were free. I wondered if this was some non-verbal reaching-out cue on this woman's part, penance for being the only person who had not returned *any* of my smiles in the halls so far.

I slid my tray onto the table with a glance in her direction. In this arid social setting, a mere peek my way would have seemed a feast. Instead my table mate, apparently a highly advanced master in the art of Going Within, stared through and past me to the Stations of the Cross without the slightest shift in energy that the nearness of another person normally prompts. Her face a blank, she worked her way through a hot dog and chips, then turned her attention to chocolate ice cream, all without the slightest psychic hint that anyone else was present.

I sat in shock, nullified, sick with hurt feelings and with uncharitable thoughts. Were solitude and silence so all-consuming here that even a glance or the gesture of politely moving a lunch tray a few inches to accommodate another tray could not be indulged? *Who in their right mind goes on retreat to pretend forty other people aren't there?* Would St. Ignatius honestly approve?

I lingered in the heat after Going Within had left the table. A fly explored my picked-over lunch while the chocolate ice cream melted to an unctuous brown pool. My day was ruined. Verily, Going Within had ruined my entire *life*. But then, why not? Nowhere is it written that everything should be as I like. If the ruining of a day or a life is in progress, at least that means *something* is happening around here.

St. Philo of Alexandria's wonderful little saying came to mind: "Be kind, for everyone you meet is fighting a great battle." There; I must not judge. My table companion must have flown in from another country where they don't know any better. Or she just lost someone she loves. Maybe she's blind. Anything but to accept that I was not worth acknowledging on any level over hot dogs and ice cream under a cottonwood tree.

I had a small melt-down in the spiritual director's office later. I whispered out my bewilderment over the scenario at lunch through a constricted throat, astonished at how disappointed I am with the format of this retreat, unable to make my peace. The counselor listened, but didn't seem to find the woman's behavior odd. She's very zen, this lady. She suggested I borrow art supplies from her office and draw my feelings on paper. When people want you to draw a picture of your feelings, you know you've been found wanting.

Later: *Lord Jesus Christ, Have Mercy on Me.* I sat in the scalding air under a tall maple and watched people wander the grounds, some dangling a rosary, some staring over the plains below the mesa as heat wrinkled the air around them. It fits here, this wandering I see so much of.

Writer Gretel Ehrlich asserted that "to know something then, we must be scrubbed raw, the fasting heart exposed." Here in the terrifying silence we're offered the chance to discover how minute is a man or woman. It is the sort of thing people discover about themselves while stranded in elevators. When the clutter is removed, when we're confined to a space either restrictive or terrifyingly vast, our intrinsic nakedness is exposed, life seen raw and tender; this vanity of vanities.

In silence we must actually face ourselves. Though we are grounded by God, we still wander within the enormity of our calling to not only know but *become* like God. Because our hearts are often cold, it's difficult even to *like* God at times, let alone love Him. He's endless, holy, loud in His silence. By contrast, we stand sweating under a tree dangling a rosary, with every heartbeat and breath at His mercy. Like Abraham, Isaac and Jacob, we can be but wanderers before the Lord, clinging with faith to that mercy. No wonder modern people stay so busy. It's hard to be with God.

I cried watching them, these others that I'll never know, struggling apart from me yet with me in the heat, trapped within the contradictory color and bleakness of their earthly lives. *Lord Jesus Christ, Have Mercy on Me.*

Day Four:

Every morning now, I consider the lilies. Old blooms whither, new ones swell to golden wonders. In the heat, the roses are heavy with scent – coral and scarlet, pink as cheeks. Today I read about birds from a big, detailed book I found in the library. This is the first scholarly curiosity I've ever had about birds. The robin family helps me muster gratitude as I exert effort to appreciate the empty slate of this new day. I'd be healthier here if I had some small occupation, some outlet for service. The monks know this. In monasteries, contemplation is balanced with work. Thomas Merton, no stranger to contemplation, wrote that the humble person seeks silence not in inactivity but in ordered activity, proper to who he is before God. I'm half regretting I didn't dig into St. Ignatius at the outset. All that counting of "G----" would have given me something to do.

At lunch I felt real charity toward the other diners, and some release from the self-imposed hurt of imagined jabs and rejections. All live here alone, I must remember. All must daily manage the yawning commodity of time. All have long, hot hours ahead, holed up with Bibles and journals in stuffy rooms or the slightly cooler house lounge or out on the almost unbearably hot grounds. It would appear I've adjusted to the fact that nobody's talking around here.

I pulled out *Sense and Sensibility* against the sluggish movement of the sun across the sky. I'm astonished how out of place Elinor is here. Only yesterday she was sage to the world, her words sparse and wise, one of Austen's premier stoic heroines. Here, she seems to chatter incessantly.

There was a new guy in the buffet line at dinner. What a novice! Wide-eyed and unsuspecting, he chatted to no one in particular on the novelty of seeing raisins at a salad bar. Everyone ignored him of course, thoroughly occupied with lofty matters as they spooned up rice pilaf.

When small tongs from the salad bar fell to the floor, the new guy retrieved them, handing them to me with what seemed like unnecessarily in-depth commentary.

And lo, I didn't know what to say. Beaten about the head and shoulders by silence for four days has apparently rendered me mute in a crisis. With a forced smile and barely audible *thank you*, I placed the tongs reverently among the cheese cubes. The interaction represented a brief, hopeful window of contact with the old life, the old ways that lie just beyond this mesa, an entire world of people using up thousands, millions of delicious, comforting words all day, carrying on about any old thing at all without a thought to the preciousness of normal human interaction.

I watched the new guy consuming his dinner in bafflement at a table of Stepfords, trying to engage someone, anyone, in light conversation. The Jesuits must have forgotten to go over the rules. How terrifying it must have been at bedtime when he realized he couldn't bolt his door against us.

Day Five

It's Sunday, and there was a certain dash to peoples' clothes at breakfast that under normal circumstances one might have been tempted to call a "festive touch". I was working on a second piece of toast with grape jelly when one of the Jesuits walked in and made a brisk announcement, something about keeping curtains closed on the east side of the building to block out the morning sun. The toast stuck in my throat. A human voice – rapturous as the new guy's at the salad bar last night – was speaking into the fierce silence, thick with its snooty cello music. Just as briskly, the Blessed Announcer of the Banal left the room, and it should be noted that no lightening struck him for his verbal audacity.

Come back! Come back and announce more fascinating housekeeping details into this hotbed of gnosticism! Announce all day if you want! I'll pour another cup of coffee and you can spend the next hour instructing us to separate the recyclables, shake out bath mats, tip-toe in the lobby, keep a stiff upper lip, anything.

He didn't come back. The ache in my spine that has increased since I've been here now felt as though the three blind mice had taken to skittering up and down its length. The pressure of this experiment is altering my body chemistry; the stress of such strict self-control gnawing at a deep place within I didn't know existed. This is far worse than going without food.

To make matters worse, the vicious, haunting insomnia I live with has gotten even worse the past few days. So I'm experiencing both extreme sleep deprivation and a form of solitary confinement, two of the cruelest forms of torture known to humanity. I considered refusing to be quiet any more. Instead, I had another cup of decaf and kept my mouth shut.

Afternoon: I've gotten to know the cows here. Apparently the center leases much of its property as grazing land to a rancher. A small herd of about fifteen cows, almost as many calves and the requisite grouchy bull lumber up the trails a couple of times a day to imbibe at a water tank just over the barbed wire where I like to read on a lawn chair. Members of the herd drink deeply from the tank, flick their tails around the salt lick and stand patiently chewing cud while calves suckle or frolic.

It is inspiring, the acquiescence of these cows to what they were created for. They ask for and expect nothing else. And they couldn't speak English if they tried, so I'm not offended by their silence. Most importantly, the cows are staring fixedly across the barbed wire at *me*. *Somebody* around here is paying attention to *me*. Who could imagine the day I'd be so desperate I'd treasure every placid gaze from a herd of bovines.

Later in the Lounge: Once again, I don't get it. What is the point of going on silent retreat to sit in a big room with other people and read the *Denver Post*? But this is what so many are doing tonight, and every night for that matter, comfy as can be. And *this* activity is so profound that no one's reverie ought to be disturbed? Anyway you cut it, reading the *Denver Post* is not an inward-going activity.

Maybe if Vatican II hadn't truncated the richness of the entire Catholic liturgical pattern they wouldn't have to hold these retreats to ramp up everybody's spiritual life. Judgmentally, I burrow further into Thomas Merton's *The Seven Storey Mountain*. I especially like this part, where he writes that even after months of living the cloistered life, at the very moment he was taking his final monastic vows, he admitted to not having a clue what living the contemplative life meant. So there.

I consider extroversion. Extroverts don't mind solitude per se, yet we derive our energy from people. No matter how hard I've tried to be fascinated with my inner goings-on these past days, and even with the encouragement of St. Theopan, the people around me continue to interest me more. I've even made up new names and identities for some of them, having forgotten their real names since the introductions that first night, long months ago now.

First, across the lounge reading the *Post* is one of the young men who has been here close to thirty days, the actor Matt Damon. Near Matt sits the intellectual/stand-up comedian, who I've a hunch I'll be able to catch down at a club in Denver next weekend. And over by the fireplace reading a chunky book on theology sits the dashing Latino man, a drug cartel in the Matt Damon movie I'm writing a screenplay for.

In addition, there's the Precious Gramma contingency, a smattering of Santa Clauses, Lady Who Has Nothing to Prove, Nuns Who Mourn the Veil, Kindly Professor, Richard Foster Addict, Slim and Stylish Power Walker with iPod in Withering Heat, and my old nemesis, the lady at the table-for-two, Master in Art of Going Within.

Finally, in walks the jolly man in the beret, swinging his walking stick; we'll call him Fritz. Every retreat, silent or not, needs a Fritz. The deep wrinkle between his eyes tells me he misses his yodeling. As annoying as their apathy toward me has been, tonight I feel another rush of love.

And me? Call me Done Before I Even Started. Maybe one day I'll discover some glorious purpose in this suffering. It isn't the silence itself, it's the torment of distraction. I once spent four days completely alone at our remote retreat center in rural France when the rest of the staff was away for some reason. I got a lot done in four days, and hardly thought about being alone. I am much lonelier here than I remember being then.

At sunset the sky is fire and gemstones. I wrap its beauty around my heart in this end-of-day ritual. The air around me blues to sapphire, the sky recedes into infinity. A couple of rabbits appear out of the brush and take up their ritual of playful jumping and twitching of tails. My emotions crash again when they disappear into the darkness, and loneliness engulfs me. I'm weary of this.

Day Six (Last Day):

In thin blue light before dawn this last morning I discovered a hollow of soft dirt on a patch of the property I hadn't explored yet. It is possibly a former dump, judging from a few old tires poking through. It is void of plant life except for a few white prickly poppies, a paradoxical flower with its thorny stem, barbed leaves, and translucent white flowers of exquisite delicacy atop the jarring mangle. The jet-white petals are like shots of purity in the inhospitable climate of the dump. I wept for the innocent prickly poppy ravaged by the Fall. To walk redeemed and pure in the sterile hollow of the world is the pilgrimage no Christian can escape.

At breakfast, the robin's nest was empty. The babies really were grown up enough to fly away forever, and so they have. Even the parents are nowhere to be seen. But never mind. I'm not as devastated by this odd environment as I was. My people-hungry heart has atrophied, like the stomach as a fast progresses. And maybe my inner life with God has expanded. Nothing that would take anyone's breath away, but appropriate to the person I am.

I had a last short session with my director. I have apparently gotten so used to living without the resonation of my own voice that – cross my heart and hope to die – I sounded exactly like Donald Duck. I quacked my way through the brief meeting and noticed my lips felt like Donald's too, stiff and beak-like. Come to think of it, my legs also looked like the duck's, sticking straight out from the chair. I think I have started to lose touch with my body's relationship to things around it. If I'd been on the eight-day program, I might have ended up donning a little sailor suit.

Afternoon: It's all in one's perspective, these nuggets that find their way into the gold pan of life. Not long after lunch, a rain shower blew in. The cool, pelting cloudburst washed the air of its stubborn midsummer heat, leaving a double rainbow in the aftermath of sky the color of slate. I wouldn't have known about the jeweled thing over our heads if Lady With Nothing to Prove hadn't crashed silently into the lounge to mime the rainbow to a group of us who were gazing out the French doors at the retreating storm. Lady herded us soundlessly onto the damp lawn where a bombastic Kindly Professor accosted us, a man very clearly in the throes of throwing caution to the winds.

"Rainbows, two of them!" he rasped in a bold, desperate whisper of joy as he pointed to the two arcs of unusual vividness. And off he trotted to fetch his camera.

One of the Santas stood on the grass with hands in his pockets and tears in his eyes, a smile lighting his rosy face. Matt and a young cohort were required to be cool, blinking casually into the expanse. The intellectual/stand-up comedian stood a pace off observing the scene, no doubt collecting material for his next gig. Kindly was back in a flash with the camera, barely able to restrain himself from cavorting like a schoolboy. There on the lawn we silent ones finally met each other while gazing with a single happiness at the blessed thing arched in the heavens. In those few moments, there was enough eye contact and human warmth to satisfy even me. It was a rewarding culmination to my journey into the far and lonely reaches of myself.

At twilight I slipped out of the house and threw my bag into the car I hadn't come near in six and a half days. I'd intended to take one last roam along the back trails, to say a formal goodbye to my cows and take in another sunset. But the cows were nowhere to be found, and the thought of walking those isolated stretches one more time was too doleful to endure. I drove away with the radio turned up loud; the voice of a hyperactive talk show host was auditory ambrosia. The usual tense commentary on the politics of the day had never sounded so good. Even the commercials were a feast. I couldn't get enough noise.

At home I babbled at everyone in sight through Donald Duck lips, soaking in familiar human parameters and the love of family. When I hugged Olivia's small, warm body close I felt something like a transfusion, and the three blind mice deserted my spine.

For a long time after I returned, I paid close attention to my thoughts and actions for clues to what my time on silent retreat that stifling week had meant. But a haze of bewilderment still lies over my analysis of the experience. I can't confidently effuse on the certain benefits of such a pilgrimage and its off-setting dichotomy: the pressure to reach ardently toward God all alone while miraculously restraining curiosity in the constant presence of people who were arbitrarily off limits.

But what is one pilgrim's psych ward is another's Elysian Fields. I'll always be curious about what others in my group gleaned from that time. Besides the moment we enjoyed a double rainbow together, I'll never know.

I have no regrets. I lived each moment of those six summer days out of the person I was at the time. Whether the time will ultimately prove productive or wasteful to the advancement of my soul, I can't be the judge.

I've made my peace with the paths that took me seemingly nowhere and back through that enigmatic, emotional labyrinth, twisting and turning everywhere I wouldn't have chosen to go in the first place. And yet, I did choose it. I went into the silence fairly certain I wouldn't know what to do with myself, and my instincts were correct. But I went all the same, and stayed to the end. Best to leave it be, to let sleeping cows lie, out on the hill among the sage and scrub oak, as the last faded ribbons of sunset are lost to night.

CHAPTER 6: The Journey to Standing Ground

For this is the craft of the devil...he leads us about in all directions, wandering, not having any standing ground.
St. John Chrystostom, homily VII

Terse gusts of a hot desert wind mourn through bare window openings high above me. I stand in waning daylight among a cluster of nuns and pilgrims in the cement block skeleton of a new Byzantine-style church. We are motionless and attentive to the rise and fall of quickly chanted Compline prayers echoed against walls almost three stories high. There is a peaceful pathos in these words lifted to God and mingled with the hum of wind in the roof trusses. The wind smells of hot stone, of air blown miles across terrain that is spartan of life, and of a vague, struggling greenness wafting out of the desert. The soft folds of the nuns' habits riffle in the burnt air that swirls through every opening of the sketchy frame as the sun sinks into the mountains miles away.

At the front of the church, an icon of Jesus Christ rests on an easel, in this temple to honor All Saints. The icon of the Lord looks minute, vulnerable in the cavernous nave, not unlike His state when He came to earth in the flesh as a human infant. But His power radiates out of Compline, the Church's communal prayers before sleep. It is composed of Psalms, the Doxology, the Nicene Creed, and litanies and prayers to the Mother of God.

The Compline prayers are unyielding to the world's fashion cycles of heresy, appeal to religious emotion or the lethal lull of relativism. The chanter moves into the Creed, and the tenets of my faith ring out sound and strong, stained with the blood of countless martyrs. On the Creed, this powerhouse of doctrine, the Church stands. Upon this citadel of truth Christians throughout the world bet their lives every day. And this evening as every evening, the sisters of the monastery I'll call St. Nikolai's, lay down their lives once again.

When Compline is over, the nuns and their sojourning guests thread toward the icon to make veneration. My throat constricts as I make my *metania* and kiss the edge of the icon. My piteous state before God's holiness hits me hard. We leave the gray sketch of church in silence, faces to a sunset that seems to span the entire circumference of horizon above the mountains that ring this valley. The nuns will finish chores among their goats and orchards, then retire to individual cells to rest until sometime after midnight when private prayers begin well before morning services at dawn.

It is inspiring to participate in the daily cycle of prayer in a monastery. It can also be jolting; this schedule goes against the natural laziness deeply ingrained in most human beings. Monasticism is not an easy road. But for those who are called, the monastery setting becomes the place where life opens up before willing eyes, opens a door through which a person may step into a deeper experience of God than most believe they would have found "in the world."

During my time at St. Nikolai's, I sensed acutely that monasticism is a solid path for reclaiming the "standing ground" God intended all human beings to posses, a firm foundation on which the human personality can position itself and flourish. Nothing particularly overt occurred to bring this impression to the forefront, for monasteries are generally not the territory of speculation, debate or much talk. The nuns simply lived out their days before me in prayer and obedience. In the process, peace and the goodness of their choice became my own modeled expectation.

This is not to suggest that the ground of human personality is reclaimed without sweat and struggle, without utter relinquishment. A friend who became a monk about seven years ago says this: "In my development as a newly-illumined (chrismated person), the services at church were usually long enough, just not frequent enough. I found myself envying the depths of wisdom, love and prayer that I found in books written by monks and nuns. I wanted what they had and figured the only way for me to get it was to follow their path and go monastic." Or as Mother Cassiana had put it: "It had to be all or nothing".

It is not only the monastics that benefit from this. Historically, the monastery was the place where groups of people, including entire extended families, went frequently for spiritual refreshment. One of my daughters' godmothers is a Romanian woman in her 30's. She recounts pilgrimages with her grandmother as a teenager, when thousands of people congregated at one particular monastery for four days every August for the Feast of the Dormition. This grand exodus to the country took place in full view of the local communist police who by the mid 80's had mostly thrown up their hands trying to control "the opiate of the masses" that communist ideology and pressure had worked so hard to eradicate in Romania. In many countries, the spiritual pilgrimage is still considered a kind of vacation and undertaken as a matter of course, while the parish church back home is regarded as the fixed, steady place where one partakes consistently of the Sacraments.

During the four days I spent at St. Nikolai's, I drank in the rarified atmosphere where God and the saints are intensely honored, where visitors have the chance to spread things out on the table before God and to consider life. It was the sort of place my heart seems constantly to seek. The nuns there are involved in various cottage industries to sustain the community and have abundance to offer their many visitors. They keep goats, tend vines, groves and orchards, press olive oil and cultivate a large vegetable garden from which they derive their own food, year round. Like most monasteries, they also manage a well-stocked bookstore and mail-order business.

Enormous stretches of the desert in that part of the country are still relatively untamed. The nuns must share the vast miles that surround the grounds with the likes of scorpions, rattlesnakes, coyotes, and Halloween-quality tarantulas. The vastness of the land is part of the encompassing psychological and spiritual atmosphere of the monastery. One is reminded everywhere of isolation and retreat, of being spirited to a world apart. The silence at dawn is unutterable, the austerity intentional, part of a time-tested pattern to enhance spiritual growth through the mood of the land. Similar to the philosophy of the American Amish, Orthodox monastics keep laxity in check by welcoming physical hardships. They welcome this *podvig*, this joyful struggle, for it is a known fact that the condition of one's soul is often affected by that of the body.

Three friends and I had arrived in mid-evening of the previous day, in the humid wake of the latest monsoon, a dramatic-sounding reference to the violent thunderstorms that sweep this part of the country in midsummer. We were wooden and silly after a long day on the road, tired of the same Windam Hill CD and bags of bright orange junk food we'd passed around the car all day. At the isolated turnoff for St. Nikolai's, we pulled off into the sand. Here we changed out of shorts and sandals into the long skirts and head coverings required for female visitors.

Studying my friends, I was sure I'd invited the right people. I'd asked Candice first because she unfailingly agrees to accompany me whenever adventure beckons; not everyone has a friend who is the living embodiment of spontaneity. Rebecca is everyone's middle sister, insouciant and accommodating. She has an excellent memory that enabled her to mentally archive all the relics we venerated on our pilgrimage. Charlotte is an ideologue like me, and a mother of six who trains for triathlons in her free time. I have solid histories of trust with each of them.

Candice inquired of the group whether she looked like a side of beef in her monastery outfit. She had been the one most concerned that her appearance in "big clothes" would inspire universal hilarity. Ironically, the clothes transformed her. The soft swish of long, flowery skirts and the drapings of silky scarves suited her, giving her an almost other-worldly look, as though the added protection around her body cut her off from the weary bombardment of earthly existence, bringing out a trait hidden until now. Although I didn't look as flowing as Candice, I felt something of this too as I flattened the wide scarf over my head.

In the middle of our fashion metamorphosis, two teenage boys balanced impressively on a motor scooter clearly designed for one, careened out of the brush on a narrow, rutted path and circled the car a couple of times. Then they ground back into the desert and disappeared as if by magic, along with the noise. It was then that we noticed the silence, complete and pervasive. It jogged a memory of a car trip through Death Valley as a child. My father had stopped along the lonely highway, where we were told to get out of the car and listen. The silence was so complete that we could hear our own ears ringing.

We entered the monastery grounds and parked. The reddening sky had deepened, transforming our surroundings. All was impossibly still. Immediately came the impulse to tiptoe, to whisper, to be sober and tidy. The community had just finished saying Compline and the sisters walked serenely across the property to their rest in the shadowed end of day, the folds of their habits catching gracefully in the breeze.

A young nun approached us. She was the guest mistress who would be our guide and liaison during our stay. Immediately I was drawn to her eyes, wide and clear in a lovely face. The habit focuses all one's attention on the face, for since the rest of the body is draped in yards of fabric, all the monastic presents of her physical self to the world goes out from the countenance. Though she was gentle and friendly, an inner concentration on something else was immediately evident. I noticed the prayer rope tangled in her fingers, which she constantly worked as we talked. The abbess had met her when she was not yet a teenager. "I saw a nun in her even then."

Our soft-spoken guide led us to the guest quarters, pointing out the neatly made beds around a central hearth, a table for eating and study, a small bathroom and kitchen off the main room. She communicated all she needed to and nothing more, though she laughed in all the right places at our exuberant chatter. She seemed content with her job as guest mistress. All "jobs" within a monastic community are referred to as *obediences*. A monastery is not a democracy; the men and women who submit themselves to the monastic struggle are fully aware of this when they are tonsured. The abbess or abbot of each community prayerfully decides what each member is suited to, all toward the ultimate goal of the salvation of that person's soul. These spiritual mothers and fathers consider themselves responsible to God for much of the outcome of the lives of those under their care.

It grates against our modern sensibilities, but over the centuries that such traditions have been honed, many have found this path of obedience and submission to the authority of another, one of the keys that frees them from the passions that plague earthly life, the ego that smothers potential. The monastic finds herself in a state of *fuga mundi*, an "anti-community" within the world where her life is no longer her own.

This is not to say that the Church has fundamentally different expectations of its monastics as opposed to the laity. In Orthodox Christianity, it is all one story, one search for God, one soulful trek on the journey to solid standing ground. It is the externals that take different shapes. The monastic embraces chastity, poverty and prayer. The layperson struggles among the conflicting duties and temptations of secular life. Both paths are intended to build the image of Christ within. The Church's role is to unite all to Christ.

As she left, the guest mistress reminded us to keep doors to the outside closed at all times; scorpions there apparently have a fondness for indoor reprieves. And about that basket of plastic whistles on the hearth; we were to wear one around our necks every time we went out. If we saw a rattlesnake on the grounds, we should blow the whistle and a nun would race to the scene with a net and a rifle to eliminate the problem. "It's nothing like it used to be," shrugged the nun. "We were killing them constantly in the early years." I pictured the abbess assigning target practice to novices as obediences.

Two other women shared the large room with us. One was Irena, a Romanian girl who'd been in the States only a few months, and been married only two weeks. She had met her Texan husband on an Orthodox internet site for singles. The two were making a honeymoon tour of monasteries.

"We expected this," Irena laughed when someone remarked about her being separated from her new husband every night; monasteries offer separate quarters for male and female guests, including married ones. Our other roommate, a Russian woman named Tatiana, was asleep after an exhausting two-day Greyhound excursion from the backside of Nevada. Her teenage daughter would arrive early the next morning by the same harrowing transport.

For the sake of the motionless Tatiana we tried to keep our voices down while we devoured the delicious vegetarian food the sisters had left for us, then settled into sleep. It was a restless night. My body missed the assortment of small, lumpy pillows I stuff ritually into niches against my back and belly to provide a womb-like pressure that sometimes helps keep me asleep at night.

Right on schedule at 2 a.m., my inner clock jogged me into a gravelly wakefulness. I lay bathed in the hot, achy, unnatural state; too wide awake to go back to sleep, yet exhausted and yawning. But there was the Jesus Prayer, rounds of it on my rope, punctuated with pricks of jealousy toward the even breathing I heard throughout the room. It was a long vigil. They are all long.

I must have finally dozed. I opened my eyes to a room rimmed in gray light and heard the bright, smiling peal of morning bells. A nun under the bell pavilion was fulfilling her obedience at the start of this new day. The smiling bells summoned us out to that glowing coal of spiritual verve that fuels the Orthodox faith from the core out. The call to attention, adoration and to receive the Body and Blood of Christ was irresistible, despite the sick ache of sleep deficiency in my shoulders. I trotted with the others the few paces from the guesthouse to the small log chapel where the Midnight office would soon begin.

The small chapel at St. Nikolai's is alive with gold and fire and scintillating icons. It seems a small space to contain the expansiveness that occurs in worship among these saints, this "cloud of witnesses". Icons are addictive; no matter how many are present, it's never enough.

Nuns entered with deliberate care, attention to every step as though counting each breath, and gathered on the right side of the chapel. Fully-tonsured nuns wore the long black veil that is added for church, the veil falling halfway across their faces and obscuring them from us to an even greater degree. The veil accentuates their separation from secular life, a reminder of their complete consecration to God. It is meant to help them in their process. Seeing this as a positive thing, it makes me wonder why so many of the Catholic nuns gave it up.

Each nun began to read from long, thick lists of people from around the world who have submitted names for prayer. Meanwhile, a huddle of pilgrims materialized out of the dawn; Irena with her husky Texan; a rested Tatiana and her yawning daughter fresh off the notorious Greyhound; visitors from nearby towns; a Serbian student touring monasteries in the States to study Church music; several young women who were spending anywhere from several weeks to a year among the sisters. "I'm not sure yet just why I'm here," confessed one to me afterward. She had committed for a year.

I had assumed I would be curious about the lives of these nuns, as is my wont. But as prayer enfolded me, my curiosity dissipated. I didn't need to "know" what had led so many very young women to this particular choice or what had fitted several older ones with the garb of the novice. Being present with them brought all clarity. There has to be tremendous scope for growth in this setting. I received the Eucharist and emerged into the sunshine.

"Self-hatred is a sin." The monk's bright eyes bore into mine. "It is a form of pride and must be confessed as sin. Sin is all that's wrong with us. But it's just sin, nothing more. People get intimidated by it. Don't ask so many *why's*; that's too Freudian. Just ask *what*. Name the sin specifically and confess it as such. In this way the thing loses its power. Remember; you are a sinner, not a failure. People must learn to make repentance an art. Some don't know how to repent. Christians must develop profound self-knowledge and learn to engage in effective spiritual warfare by applying counter-attack with force equal to the attack."

We had taken refuge from the searing sun in a pleasantly air-conditioned sitting room in the main monastery house. It was our good fortune that morning to have the monastery's resident priest-monk all to ourselves. We were well into the throes of ringing every morsel of insight from him that was possible before lunch.

Our new friend looked perfectly comfortable on a tiny, sateen-covered chair in the decidedly feminine sitting room. He is a big man with the easy laugh, eager wit and polished communication of one who clearly loves the company of other people. Some of the nuns do not have authorization to interact with visitors. We were learning to take nothing for granted, so our appointment with the nuns' confessor was a feast, this man who with every word and facial expression revealed he had paid his dues in the Christian struggle, and was happy to give us the benefit of his experience.

We'd met him earlier that morning as he waved cheerfully to our group from a golf cart, speeding through the center of the monastery grounds between plantings of succulents. He looked jolly, irrepressibly joyful. Had we stumbled on Santa Claus? I thought about running after him through the heat waves and demanding his autograph.

"I can tell he likes us. We can't let him get away," I said breathlessly as we watched him hop off the golf cart and enter the main house with another enthusiastic wave in our direction. We inquired, and discovered through one of the talking nuns that the Father is always happy to spend time with visitors. "With him, the more the merrier," she said. Here was an interesting idea: an extroverted monk.

"It wasn't the theology so much. I was attracted to Christianity when I met Christians who were loving," he told us. "They had a quality, a wisdom my studies in psychotherapy couldn't match. I remain a Christian because it works. If people will obey the commandments of Christ, they will *feel* the love of God in their lives."

He took us everywhere and back in that conversation, traipsing with big energetic strides across the countryside of Christian thought, theology and the practice of Christian living. He talked about the right attitude in receiving the scourging of God (nothing less than humility); identifying modesty as a virtue, not an affectation of dress; viewing ascetical practice as a way of gaining insight into another realm; recognizing spiritual gifts as mere shells of virtue. It went on for two hours. Needless to say, we took a lot of notes.

The extroverted monk sat back. "Satan doesn't bother me as much anymore. He gives up on people who counter-attack consistently." Then he leaned forward, apparently still in full sail. "Was there anything more? Have I answered all of your questions?"

A nun came into the sitting room and quietly invited us to wait on the veranda until we were ushered in for lunch. Lunch was another delicious vegetarian meal, eaten with other pilgrims in a room adjacent to the nuns' dining room. Everyone ate silently while we listened to a young nun with a sweet, sing-song voice read from a book about self-deception.

By mid-afternoon, I was desperate for a run. I had gone too long without serious exercise and was starting to pace in free moments, not a good use of pilgrimage time. The heat of the day was at its zenith. It was now or never, since Vespers was approaching. Once dinner and Compline were over, too many potentially fatal desert creatures would have emerged to make such an outing wise. I knew; the first night Charlotte and I had tried to jog the outskirts of the monastery grounds too close to dusk. True to our guide's caution, tarantulas had skittered across our path in the gloaming and cut our evening constitutional short. The scorpions couldn't have been far behind.

There was no question of donning shorts and a tee-shirt. A change out of sandals to running shoes and the protection of my wide-brimmed hat would have to suffice to get me about two Sabbath day's journeys into the desert in my wieldy skirt; just enough to churn up some endorphins. The sun had gone behind a substantial cloud – the blessed thing – as I trotted up the dirt road that slices through untamed desert on either side. A few drops fell, then a light shower, then the clouds evaporated and the sun was again merciless. I concentrated on the road, rubber soles on hard-packed dust, and on the silence that stung my ears when I stopped to mop my face with a red bandana. A person could explode in such heat, I thought. But addiction trumps heatstroke.

The desert should not be pitied. Only a pampered perception judges such a place needy, the human tendency to recoil from what is not ample, lush, even excessive. Plants here naturally distance themselves from each other in the competition for moisture. When the rain does come, it suffices the comical teddy-bear cholla, prickly pear, saguaro and scrappy shrubs. Most of these can survive years without moisture if they must. This lean outback that is sensorily austere is a reminder our souls and bodies need far less from earthly surroundings than we think. To insist on more than presents itself naturally through God's provision is to squander life-energies designed to be satisfied in simplicity, which has its own allure.

In the silence I grasped briefly why so many saints of the past chose the desert. The desert is a place of fasting; the unyielding vastness, the discomfort, even the deadliness of the desert offer a restful emptiness out of which God may speak. An anonymous Desert Father wrote: "Thus is it with the man who dwelleth with men, for by reason of the disturbance caused by the affairs of the world he cannot see his sins; but if he live in the peace and quietness of the desert he is able to see God clearly."

That evening the moment of reckoning came, when girls on pilgrimage for the higher good and the sake of *podvig* must sublimate their horror of oversized

bugs that can actually kill a person. Three of us lay
peacefully on our beds after Compline while Candice
rummaged for something in her suitcase. Not two inches
from her hand, a tarantula as big as a tea saucer clung
casually to the wall – the rascal had made it through The
Door That Ought to Remain Shut. Candice emitted the
requisite scream, sent a handful of travel-size toiletries
into the air and receded to a corner, all with thespian
precision. I would have joined her, but it still remained
that a spider sporting hidden fangs and possibly packing
a chain saw was squatting with great pomp and ugliness
on our wall. Who knows what color body fluids might
course through his hairy self, to deter my smashing him
with a shoe.

I grabbed a clear salad bowl from the kitchen,
clapped it over the intruder and slid a dinner plate
underneath. One revolting segment of brown leg caught
under the edge of the bowl. I passed the spider-under-
glass to Rebecca, who walked twelve paces into the
twilight where she tossed the entire thing into the yucca
and ran. "The nuns say they jump," she said with a
shiver. We hoped we wouldn't rue the day of our mercy.

Candice gradually recovered. She passed a broom
under all the beds and probed into corners to ferret out
the dozen or so remaining tarantulas that *must* be lurking.
She unpacked and repacked her suitcases. She implored
us to do the same. But after a day of sweating, soul
searching, standing in multiple services, a torrid jog,
more sweating and now an encounter with the stuff
haunted houses are made of, I had no energy for such
fervency. For once, someone else was doing the
worrying normally assigned to me, the reflexive pessimist
in any group. What a luxury to let another exorcise the
remaining critters. I crawled between the sheets with no

thought for what my feet might find at the bottom, and slept like the dead until 2 a.m.

In the spring of 7th grade, one of my classmates was struck by a car on the street in front of our school. Among other things, a head wound left what seemed like a great deal of the girl's blood on the asphalt until the ambulance could arrive. For days after the accident, a browning stain marked the place where Mickey had sprawled motionless that day, tainting the street and stalking the minds of we who knew her from math class and crowded halls. Long after the drama of the accident had worn off as a topic of lavatory chatter, I'd still walk cautiously past the unattended spot on Iliff Avenue, confirming that the place was still branded by blood that had once moved warm inside a young body.

On these pilgrimages, nausea closed over me and I shook inside. I grappled with a miracle; a girl just my age could have died, but mercifully had not. Sometimes bad things that should happen, don't. Though I couldn't have articulated it, a primitive understanding of the words *grace* and *mercy*, heard so often in church, was taking shape in my spirit. Mickey's blood became a metaphor for things I'd never had to consider before: life was fragile – Mickey's life and mine – and the lives of every student in our troubled school, a flagship for Denver's budding racial desegregation policies. Mickey's blood – this strange conceit – marked the dawning of adult self-consciousness, the shedding of the chrysalis of my childhood. I would be baptized a Christian within a year.

Long afterward, I would stand in the chapel at St. Nikolai's on the fifth morning of our sojourn in the desert, eyes gullied in tears as they had been every morning that week when the priest appeared on the solea with the precious chalice carefully covered by a red napkin – life-giving color of the Holy Mysteries. To be present in that chapel was a miracle. I could have died in my sins long ago, but had not. By some marvel that should never have occurred but had, the kindness of God was alive in the world. It was available to me, the sinner. Every morning in that desert chapel, grace gushed from an unseen source to flood the normally sullen, shadowed crevices of my heart and fill me first with intense gratitude, and finally with the Body and Blood of God Himself.

Few single things in life change us profoundly. It is far more often one's daily, hourly choices that make the difference; incremental exposure to good or evil, beauty or obscenity, substance or void, that culminates in the person we each will be in the end. We are image-bearers of God and will – God willing – grow in the authenticity of that image by diligent exposure to the very best we are able to access in this world. Pilgrimage among holy things and people who face steadily into the Light is part of that very best. Through each contact with such channels of God's grace, we inch forward in our heart's journey. Along the way, we may catch brief glimpses of a broad, open day ahead that spurs us on; a thin ray of uncreated light, a gossamer rainbow of expectation, or the muted, far-off beat of dove's wings near a throne where Love waits.

CHAPTER 7: It Hides a Well

What makes the desert beautiful is that somewhere it hides a well.
Antoine de Saint-Exupéry

I've always wanted to pilgrimage to Mount Athos in Greece. But I'm getting ahead of myself. More accurately, I never gave Mount Athos a second thought until a few years ago when I was made to understand that I could never, ever set foot on this mountainous 250-mile peninsula jutting into the Aegean Sea for the simple reason that I was a female.

In this day and age it is a startling thing to be disallowed somewhere for being a girl. But then, Mount Athos is a startling and enigmatic place. The folks who call it home are a single-minded, highly spiritual lot, not much given to notions of political correctness. They've paid their dues in ascetic hardship and the pursuit of God over the past 1500 years. It has paid off, for today Mount Athos is considered none other than the glittering spiritual epicenter of the Christian world. As even Adolf Hitler could tell you, this is not a peninsula to be trifled with.

One website, inathos.gr, declares the Holy Mountain to be "the only place in Greece that is completely dedicated to prayer and worship of God." I can only imagine what the inhabitants of other monasteries on other Greek peninsulas make of such an assertion. Be that as it may, people who visit describe it as an experience like no other, a harbor of unnatural peace, incubator of the miraculous. Its twenty male monasteries and numerous sketes and hermitages have been an irresistible draw to pilgrims from around the world for centuries, and thousands still visit every year, including such luminaries as the Prince of Wales.

But every one of those visiting thousands is a man. This despite the fact that the Orthodox Church credits the Virgin Mary, its most revered saint, with the original prophesy for Mount Athos as a center for prayer. With her high credentials, you'd think the Mother of God would be an entrance ticket for other women.

But that's the irony of Athos. The Mother of God is revered so highly by the Athonite monks that they take precautions against distraction from this devotion. With a few wartime exceptions when women and girls were sheltered in the monasteries from the Turks or Nazis, and not counting the few ornery females who occasionally wash up on the beach in bikinis, women are strictly forbidden from setting foot in Port Dáfni.

I can grudgingly understand this restriction. Guys in general like to protect their men-only gatherings and activities; cigars were invented for this purpose. In the case of Mount Athos, it must be remembered that its residents are breathtakingly intent on what the Orthodox call "the path to salvation", referring to one's journey toward God and becoming like Him. According to rumor, women are notorious for putting up sneaky, unauthorized detour signs along this path to salvation, sending unsuspecting travelers off on every sort of wild goose chase. Being men, the detoured ones categorically refuse to ask for directions back to the right path. Better to eliminate such humiliating possibilities entirely by just keeping the girls *out*.

This ban on females makes Mount Athos the ultimate "NO GURLS ALOWD" tree house, though hopefully without the BB guns sometimes found in such establishments. Just consider the ensuing chaos if a woman did show up on the welcome mat at one of the monasteries, after all these years of male exclusivity.

Faithful to her sex, she would quickly ascertain that a woman's touch was badly needed around the place, and begin to tidy up. This would simply not do on the Holy Mountain, all this wielding of lilac-scented air freshener and scraping of stepladders to measure the windows for floral valences. In reaction to such sissy stuff, out would come the BB guns, and the Greek media would have a field day.

That's where St. Anthony's Greek monastery in Florence, Arizona in the Western Hemisphere comes in, a veritable hotbed of egalitarian thinking, where male and female visitors alike can catch a glimpse of Athonite life. The monks who founded this community in the Arizona desert in the early 1990's came from the Holy Mountain itself. One hot day six of them started digging wells among the saguaro, and fourteen years later looked up to notice they'd carved out Paradise. "This place is pretty," they must have decided. "Girls should see it, too."

Friends of mine who had visited St. Anthony's and tried to describe it to me seemed universally at a loss for words. They'd pale, their eyes would roll back in their heads while they'd gasp out, "I dunno… I dunno." With trembling hands a few of them produced photos of something like a botanical garden on steroids, a tangle of luminous, celery-colored tropical ferns, stately palms and riotous subtropical flowers; a stunning, fluorescent cocoon of Edenic beauty in which human subjects in the pictures appeared as bewildered, washed-out specks among the colossal herbage. Decoratively tiled fountains, icon shrines and half a dozen lavish churches and chapels also graced the pictures. This was a place perfectly, faultlessly lovely, where anyone might worship in the glorious traditions of the Orthodox Church, and bask in the innocence of Eden on the off hours.

The original plan to visit St. Anthony's had seemed a smashing one, replete with visions of myself and three steady friends bashing around the Sonoran desert in our head coverings and silver and turquoise Indian jewelry. We would sketch cacti in our journals and pray before relics day and night. Even God would be surprised at how resourceful we were with our monastery time. But we had just come from St. Nikolai's, where it struck me on the long drive that day that we'd paid our dues in exertion already. My sandals worn with socks no longer looked artsy. I was tired of matted hair under the head covering. I already craved meat. By the looks on the others' faces, I doubted I was the only one who wondered if we'd bitten off more than we could chew.

We needn't have worried. There's nothing to revive flagging spirits determined to pilgrimage to the bitter end like driving ever deeper into the eccentric landscape of the American desert. The further west we traveled, the more copious the saguaro cacti became, a clearly endless forest of the odd, twisted giants bravely erect against a scorched Arizona sky. The aridity and desolation of the desert reminded us there were fresh new doses of asceticism just ahead, and this awareness somehow revived us. It is uncanny, this miracle of whimsy that lurks is the desert. By the time we rolled into the St. Anthony parking lot, I was ready for a hair shirt and shackles.

But we were late for Vespers. "Will they be mad?" someone wanted to know as we toiled through pea gravel to the main gate that opened into a flagstone patio. There we were transported into a scene whose welcoming extravagance took me by surprise, even though I'd been prepared through my friends' pictures of the place. Cooling fountains splashed and sparkled around us. Date palms and containers of flowers swayed in a slight breeze around pretty benches where pilgrims whispered quietly. The utter beauty and delicacy of the surroundings drew me immediately in. The monks of St. Anthony's may be known for their rigorous Athonite lifestyle, but they had certainly splurged on luxurious hospitality for the rest of us. This was one serious oasis, and I felt an urge to bow down to something.

The young monk who greeted us wasn't mad. Except for his monastic attire, he looked like any sweet, gangly college kid, happy we'd stopped by and not distressed at all that we appeared to be women, finding our head-to-toe swathing satisfactory. Our host suggested we leave our things in the car for now in order to pray at the end of Vespers. Afterwards, we should follow the crowd to *trapeza*, the word for mealtime in monastic lingo. I thought about the fresh fruit we'd bought at a roadside stand that morning, now simmering to pie filling in the back seat in the intense afternoon heat. But this is the way of things in monastery parking lots in the desert, when Vespers must be attended and God in His wisdom has chosen to make southern Arizona the swelter capital of the western world.

Knowing the services would be done exclusively in Biblical Greek, we'd brought along our service books in English. We needn't have bothered, for as we entered the main church, we discovered these monks like their churches good and dark, which I'd read they do on Mount Athos as well. There were no lights; a few candles glowed before the icons and on chanters' stands, obscuring human features, blurring depth and height. All was shadowed, embered; even the substance of worship muffled in the cavernous space, echo-filled with the unfamiliar language.

The chanting tones were hypnotic, bringing me present to my own breathing and the movement of my fingers over the prayer rope as I murmured the Jesus Prayer. In the soft swaddling of semi-darkness I discovered a surprising inner breadth for worship, nudged toward heavenly things as this first service of the liturgical day progressed. Already, we were living the Athos dream.

On the short walk from Vespers to the refectory, I heard almost nothing but Greek spoken by other pilgrims. When I heard English, it was often heavy with a Greek accent. I would learn that St. Anthony's is a veritable gathering place for pious Greek Americans as well as Greek-Greeks who make the long voyage overseas. Considering that Greece literally crawls with monasteries ancient and new, I wondered why so many feel the need to travel so far.

Trapeza was an amusing study in culture, with a lot of matter-of-fact pushing and jostling as diners took their places at the long tables with the innocent disregard for "personal space" I remembered from living in Mediterranean countries. The monastic brotherhood sat at a table of their own, male pilgrims squeezed in at another, while women and girls outnumbered everyone else, crowding into the benches around two tables. At the head table the abbot sat alone, a serious-looking man who ate methodically and seemed to be deep in thought or prayer.

The meal was eaten briskly, with everyone more or less fending for his or herself among the bowls of food. No one smiled warmly or patted the hands of the four shy new girls who were obviously in great need of flattery and nurture. Instead, all ears were on a monk who read out of the lives of the saints from a lectern high at one end of the room, in Greek of course.

Since my knowledge of Greek is limited to the letters of the alphabet I once taught my children, I had time to study the monks. I'd heard there were a number of younger monks in this community, and I noticed several older men in the habit worn by novices, answering God's call on their lives in that later life stage. All seemed to enjoy the meal. And why not, since they'd been working and praying hard all day.

We finished our pea soup, chunks of pungent feta cheese, watermelon and plump, home-cured green olives, then rose as a group while the abbot prayed over the throng. Monasteries leave no stone unturned when there's a chance to spiritualize an event; *trapeza* is considered a type of service in itself. The abbot and his team filed out in silence, followed by the pilgrims – men followed by women – while the abbot raised his hand in blessing to each one at the door of the refectory.

Faded evening light was at the window when I left my tired friends in our room in the women's guesthouse to explore the grounds alone. It didn't take long to understand why peoples' eyes had rolled back in their heads so consistently when they tried to describe St. Anthony's to me. Not only were the grounds stunning, but an unseen quality permeated everything; to me nothing less than the indefinable scent of God. An almost palpable spiritual aroma flooded my anxious nervous system, releasing it from the gray, cloying grip of care that so often pervades. I meandered on the flagstone paths, tensions unraveling like old yarn, trailing behind me in the dusk. Anxiety was impossible in the atmosphere of holy hush.

"And the Spirit of God brooded…"

The sun dropped under the desert; humidity from a recent monsoon held the heat close. Arriving at a far border of the monastery grounds I drank in the post card scene before me – blackened curls of saguaros in silhouette against a showy magenta sunset. A monk in a security vehicle pulled up next to me, sunglasses perched casually on his forehead. He initiated small talk about the weather, asked if I was a relative of one of the monks, and finally cautioned me not to walk into the desert at nightfall. He'd seen a mountain lion not far from this spot the previous evening.

People often exhort me like this. I must have that look about me, of someone perpetually poised to launch myself into the jaws of wild animals. In this case the monk's hunch was right; I probably would have ventured out a hundred paces to hug a saguaro or two. Perhaps this wasn't a monk at all, but an angel.

What my friends and I would jokingly refer to later as "Saturday morning hangin' around the monastery" came upon us all too quickly in its brutal disguise as the middle of the night. We crashed from our beds when the alarm shrilled at 1:45 a.m., weak and shaking, reminding each other in groggy tones of willed conviction that a pilgrimage is *not* after all, a vacation. Spiritual effort is the order of the day; solemn openness to God, grand petitions beamed forth into the night, hearts and faces set like flint toward the Mystery of He Who Worketh As He Willeth. If getting there included church on the backside of midnight, we were game.

The night air was balmy; soft breath against my skin. A full moon in an aura of haze shone between date palms that swayed in the kind nocturnal breeze. In the air was a distinctive tang, almost like the ocean. How close to Baja were we, anyway? We padded quietly through the maze of flagstone walkways to find the Midnight Office in full swing. A wall of incense-laden darkness draped around us. We groped our way to the icons for veneration and found seats on the women's side.

I decided to try one of the *stasidia*. These are partly enclosed wooden seats monastery churches sometimes offer, with a system of raising or lowering a small platform that allows the worshipper to stand, sit, or lean. I was to try all three positions throughout the weekend on this concerted fast from comfort and can only say I'm glad the monks find them helpful.

Happily, during services of such reverence and intensity, the comforts of the body recede in importance. We celebrated the Eucharist as gray light replaced the night, then stepped out into a fresh summer dawn. Once again we were herded toward the refectory and jostled into place at our long tables. There we ate from bowls of remarkably cold French fries and scrambled eggs, and listened once again to the monk read in Greek from his high podium.

No one seemed to mind. The unorthodox fare suited the general atmosphere of asceticism we were encountering at every turn. I would have been far more annoyed if monks in snowy aprons had appeared at our elbows with platters of steaming waffles and omelets, somehow canceling out all the lovely spiritual work we'd just done in church. Besides, all was forgiven by the presence of more magnificent homegrown olives. With every bite I blessed the brothers who'd picked and set these juicy, colossal fruits to brine.

But I barely noticed the food anyway. I was busy falling in love, my eyes riveted to a small, elderly monk, bent and struggling to walk with a cane. His beard was snow white, his ancient face creased with the effects of a long, determined road, a narrow way. Life had forged character into his every movement. He was irresistible.

Apparently I wasn't the only one with a crush, for on the porch after *trapeza* this reverend father was immediately surrounded by children and adults alike, toward whom he smiled and nodded with a charming shyness and a few soft words in Greek, his face alight with what I guessed had something to do with massive contact with Jesus Christ over the years.

Vicki, a veteran St. Anthony's pilgrim from Toronto, explained that Fr. Gregory is what is known as a "simple monk", not a priest-monk who hears confessions. Technically, pilgrims shouldn't kiss his hand. But it was obvious that no one could resist, swarming forth with abandon to kiss the hand, come what may.

None of his admirers seemed to care *what* Fr. Gregory was technically, just *that* he was. They are compelled to be near him. Perhaps there was some special dispensation for these kissing-blessings in his case, since Fr. Gregory didn't have the look of a guy who would go around intentionally breaking important rules.

Not wanting to miss out, I marched over, bowed and touched my fingers to the ground in a *metania* and kissed the hand he extended to my cupped ones. I've read that the intent of monastics is to live "like the angels". The fact that I could barely tear myself from this one's side told me somebody was doing a pretty good imitation job. It can be known only to God what it has cost to translate an ordinary man into one who emanates such angelic freedom from ego. The rest of us glean hungrily from the shadows.

Saturday was a blur of content, this holiday into the holy. We relished every bend in the flagstones, each new marvel of nature or architecture we encountered as we wandered the grounds like damsels in a fairy tale, or more likely like four sensory-overloaded and sleep-deprived pilgrims in long, wrinkled skirts. We stood over relics and touched our prayer ropes and neck crosses to those of Mary Magdalene, St. Lazarus and St. Panteleimon – the physician-martyr who is the patron of one of my sons. We stood in the open, Norwegian stave chapel of St. Seraphim of Sarov, weeping as we said the Akathist to Our Sweetest Lord Jesus, some of the most beautiful prayers to Christ I have ever read.

Out of the dust of the Sonoran, something astounding has been wrested in that great, green oasis. Whatever it is – this sparkling spaciousness for the spirit – its effect is blatant, and changes the way people see the world and life. At St. Anthony's, I found it easy to believe heaven exits – a world beyond this one; a strong, pristine Somewhere I can obtain if I will.

Late in the afternoon we made our way up a hill on one of the far ends of the property to a sparkling, paper-white chapel in the classic Greek style often seen in travel brochures. This very day, this very Vespers, would be the first service held within the airy interior of this church dedicated to the ancient Jewish prophet Elias.

The chapel was bursting to capacity; surely someone had gone out into the highways and byways to bring in fresh recruits for the occasion. And in the style I have so often observed in ethnic Orthodox churches, few people stood still as though they were in fact *in church,* but divided and multiplied throughout the service like a group of cells, coming and going with much exhortation to their fellows to make more room for the constant influx of more worshippers. Young mothers in bright scarves who'd carried heavy children up the hill, workmen from a nearby road construction site, sprightly bent Greek *Ya Yas* in black, leaning heavily on their canes; all seemed perfectly at ease with the revolving door atmosphere which I might add, subtracted greatly from the effect of the chapel's air conditioning unit.

The stamina of these Greeks amazed me. No one but a rapidly wilting Candice and myself seemed the slightest bit ruffled by the heat or the crowd or by the clearly endless number of candles in large hanging candelabras that apparently *must* be lit for an inaugural Vespers in a white chapel on a hill. Had I fainted away from the rigors of the evening, there would have been nowhere to sink dramatically to the ground. There I would have stood in my unconscious state until the multitude finally broke up to tear down the hill to *trapeza*.

But it was worth it. Someday when I bring my yet-unborn grandchildren on pilgrimage to St. Anthony's in the interminable heat of an Arizona summer, I will point up the hill to the dazzling chapel of Prophet Elias and recount in hushed tones the story of that first Vespers. To which the little tykes will wonder aloud if the monks sell popsicles down at the bookstore.

Not long after midnight on Sunday morning Rod Serling shook me awake and escorted the four of us back through the balmy air under the stars into that shadowy warp between heaven and earth where nothing seems quite real, yet strangely more solid than life anywhere else. Outside the house of worship, the sharp, jutting world receded to mere option.

We had not progressed far into the Midnight Office before Vicki from Toronto was at our sides: now would be a good time to tiptoe to the front of the church to receive a blessing from Elder Ephrém, the monastery's visionary founder. I'd been reluctant to do this the day before as I'd heard rumors of the venerable elder's clairvoyance. I feared I might receive his blessing at the precise moment my mind would be exercising some uncharitable line of thought such as, "Why they gotta make these services so long?" I also wondered if he ever gets tired of people streaming through the place in droves, probing for a hand to kiss. I didn't want to bug him.

But as I thought about it, good manners required I at least acknowledge the good elder's existence. After all, he'd gone to all that work to build the lovely fountains I'd been enjoying. The least I could do was check in and telepathically thank him.

I shuffled into the fog and located the dignified gray-bearded man in his special elder chair. I made my *metania*, kissed his hand and glanced into his face. Nothing could have prepared me for what I saw. Although quite elderly and recovering from recent surgery, Elder Ephrém appeared perfectly alert and fresh in the smoky room with four hours of church ahead of him. It would seem there was nowhere else he'd rather be but where he was, beaming on a total stranger in the middle of the night.

His look was not of polite obligation but of astonishing eagerness, as though he knew me well and was delighted to see me again. Yes, *delighted*. The impression was so potent, so unlike anything else, that I took a step back. I forgot to thank him for the fountains. There was nothing to do but return to my stall and cry for the next half hour. I willed my memory to retain the extraordinary affection I'd seen in the man, wanting to hang on forever to this reminder of Christ's love. And I grieved that such moments, when God comes near my heart in such friendly ways, usually elude me.

"I had heard of thee by the hearing of the ear, but now my eye sees…"

"Pray that you may not enter into temptation..."

During that long Sunday service in the dead of night, my struggle against sleep equaled the pangs of acute hunger. Earlier, Rebecca had made the observation that the monastery experience seems designed to break down a person's defenses. I felt it now, knowing that to come unglued within one's own body is often God's cue to reach deep inside with humility and find Him strong there. St. Macarius of Optina wrote: "One must endure darkness, faintheartedness and similar things. For God sends this for the destruction of our pride, and acquiring of humility."

I could believe it. My circadian rhythms were in anarchy, as though they'd been tumbled inside a weightlessness simulator for the past week since we began our desert sojourn at St. Nikolai's. Here in this place where only the Greek language was used, I had little to hold my mental focus. The words of the service slipped around me, an island parting the flow of a stream. A bank of monk's *stasidia* blocked most visual cues of the altar area, so occasionally I'd stand on tiptoe near a wall of visiting nuns, briefly coming present to this holiest of services through a glimpse of the celebrant's body language in the litany, the Little Entrance, the Great Entrance, moving toward the moment of Consecration and the culmination of the Eucharist.

But eventually, valor succumbed to frailty. Gravity dragged at my eyelids, consciousness trolled the murky bottoms of my vigil and I slumped into the stall. For a moment I dreamed. The looming hulk of Mount Rainier drifted up through layers of cheesecloth, a memory of climbing the risky mountain as a teenager with my father and brother.

Crampons spark against rock in the darkness before dawn as we grind over scree above Camp Muir. The sun climbs. I unzip my chartreuse parka; I am too hot yet not warm enough in the fever of overexertion. The morning is too bright, filtering into an eerie aquamarine slash of crevasse that looms deep as we edge across an ice bridge. We traverse an infinite snowfield pocked with sun cups. The grip of the ice axe brings spasms to my numbed hands; trail mix is gravel in my mouth. The world grows narrow, too narrow.

When I know there is nothing left, I stop inching toward the summit in the garish morning. There is no summit, no ascent or descent. There is only the endless mountain against a nightmare of blue-black sky. The narrow fades to gray.

Through the shroud I hear my father bark an order to Billy, to dig the stove out and make tea. My brother makes and pours the tea out, fire in a Sierra cup. I drink it under the nightmare sky pressing down against the mountain, down against a girl drugged with cold and exhaustion in a chartreuse parka.

There is sudden comfort on my front and back; Dad and Billy have unzipped their own jackets to press their warmth to mine, in the offer of their blood-life to my revival. The heat of sick-sweet tea scalds and spreads. I want only to succumb.

But I do not succumb. Not to the blue-black sky, the inferno of sunburn or the panic that washes in torrents through my chest. Something within is stronger. Out of a core of single desire, my will pushes through. It comes from a strong place; too strong even for Tahoma, the mountain of legend, to resist.

At the summit I bask at the crater's warm lip, only mildly delirious from altitude in that haloed world above the clouds, where tendrils of steam rise out of the snow.

Out of this reverie I willed myself to surface, my emotions tangled in the grip of that day long ago. I came back to pilgrimage in a monastery in the gray-green desert, and to its purpose. The priest came to the women's side with the chalice that mystically holds Christ – contained in gold. I went forward to receive, to obtain His Body under the blood-red napkin, obtain at any cost. "Make the effort," exhorted St. Basil the Great. It is not given to us to find this easy.

Vicki from Toronto was our savior while at St. Anthony's. She acknowledged our existence, led us through labyrinths of mysterious monastery protocol, assured us several times a day that we looked great in head coverings and dropped by our room with the latest bulletins of Who's Who, What's Next, and How to Figure It Out. We were inspired by her dedication to rearrange business trips from Canada to accommodate runs into St. Anthony's a couple of times a year for a blessing from her spiritual father, none other than Elder Ephrém.

"All I need is a few minutes in his presence and his blessing. This place is strong; it fortifies me to go back to the world."

I understood. In contrast to the sweet, serene spirit emanating from the abbess and nuns at St. Nikolai's, and the peaceful, homey atmosphere of the Monastery of the Protection of the Holy Virgin, the energy at St. Anthony's felt decidedly masculine, indomitable, the spiritual equivalent of building sky scrapers in Manhattan. They have the flair of a ship of holy swashbucklers – these lords of St. Anthony's. Vicki must feel this, drawing on the protection and vigor of these men of the desert.

Our new friend wanted to make sure we squeezed every opportunity out of our stay. As I sat yawning in the guesthouse kitchen after breakfast that morning, she told me directly that I should obtain the abbot's blessing if I planned to put anything in print about his monastery. Something about this brisk businesswoman made it hard to say no. I was soon swimming through a blast of midday heat into a little room off the narthex of the main church. There, a friendly secretary monk scribbled my name on a list, and within a half hour I was perched on a little stool in Elder Paisíos' office, a small miracle since there aren't many free slots in his schedule.

Elder Paisíos and Elder Ephrém work out of side-by-side offices. There they counsel and pray over their spiritual children and a continual stream of pilgrims many hours every day and far into the night on occasion, in addition to managing the monastery and caring for their own monks. Like his colleague in the next office, this elder was also known for his clairvoyance – the gift of clear sight. I felt a little uneasy as I settled myself on the stool.

The pace of this man's life showed, though his eyes were clear and piercing and he had to be younger than I had guessed from a distance. Through the veneer of his outward fatigue I sensed willingness to be present, a peaceful resignation in his gaunt features. Next to his chair was a box of the powdered anti-stress vitamin packets I give my kids before their basketball games.

The elder seemed to be sizing me up. He said nothing in greeting, only stared politely. I took this as my cue to adjust my ever-slipping head covering before babbling out my request for his blessing to write. He quietly gave it – in English with a Canadian accent – no questions asked. Then, more silence.

In my universe, silence is code for boredom. I was ready to thank him and excuse myself when on a whim I decided to take up more of his valuable time by capitalizing on the clairvoyance thing. I asked if he had any ideas as to why I've been waking up just shy of 2:00 a.m. almost every night of my adult life, unable to go back to sleep.

The silence got worse. I waited, assuming he must be impressed with the profundity of my problem and was cooking up brilliant insights to free me from that day forth from the bondage of chronic insomnia. But wait; was he *shrugging* over there? I couldn't be sure. The elder sighed, and in a barely audible voice said, "I could say a couple of prayers."

That's *it*? A couple of *prayers*? I wanted to catapult myself into his personal space and shake his holy shoulders. Instead, I nodded agreeably and knelt while he began to pray silently out of a prayer book. Immediately the energy in the room was altered. Within a few seconds I was suddenly assailed by powerful, evil thoughts that crashed into my mind, whether from within or without I couldn't tell. Panicking, I began to silently pray the Jesus Prayer. I was terrified the man would suddenly click into mind-reading mode and *hear* what I was thinking. The bombardment of evil continued. Of all the people to have around when one starts thinking their most putrid thoughts since 1986, I *would* have to pick a clairvoyant. I could barely restrain myself from tearing out of the room.

When it couldn't get any worse, the elder closed the book and I was free to bow myself out backward like a Japanese ambassador, intending to bolt the building with the Jesus Prayer at top voice until I was well out of mind-reading range. But the young secretary monk was blocking my way. One look in his eyes and I dissolved into an impromptu confession of my deep embarrassment, begging my listener to apologize profusely on my behalf if Elder Paisíos asked any questions about the scary lady with the disheveled head covering and chainsaw issues.

By the nonchalance in his voice, it would seem this monk had heard the same story every hour on the hour since he'd taken the job. He assured me these elders were accustomed to praying down the heavens into peoples' lives, which regularly brought on all the resistance from Satan that would be expected. I shouldn't be embarrassed or give the matter a second thought. All that was missing from his exhortation was a hanky pressed into my palm.

I'm usually suspicious of don't-give-it-a-second-thought advice. I reason that someday, these second thoughts might come in handy, and who are the positive thinkers of the world to discourage the rest of us from clutching them firmly to our bosoms in the interim? But that day I said, "Okay." With that release came a blast of fatigue. I exchanged my pride for a nap in the bliss of our air-conditioned room.

We had an hour before Vespers started that evening. It was still oppressively hot, but Candice, Charlotte and I craved more of the grounds. We found ourselves again on the path that leads to the pretty open chapel of St. Seraphim of Sarov, the 19th century Russian monk who is quite possibly my favorite saint, for the simple reason that St. Seraphim really, really likes me.

"I have a wish," I told my friends in the St. Anthony whisper-voice we'd all adopted since our arrival. "I'm wishing I could talk to Fr. Gregory, the little angel-monk from breakfast time. Because I am wishing this so very hard and because I am so very important, my wish is granted. I am whisked through a cloud of glitter to the chapel of St. Seraphim, where Fr. Gregory is waiting to tell me that St. Seraphim is his favorite saint, too. He blesses me and tells me that life is beautiful. He tells me that everything is going to work out fine, 'even those three really hard things that are driving you nuts, my child.' Then the two of us watch a perfect desert sunset paint the sky. The End."

Candice and Charlotte smiled politely before continuing to take 700 pictures of pink flowers. Then we rounded a corner into the clearing where the chapel of St. Seraphim is located when not in use by my imagination. There, tending the oil lamps on the altar, was Fr. Gregory. I hadn't seen a single monk along these paths during our stay, let alone *my* monk in the chapel of my favorite saint at the precise moment I was wishing for it. The old man noiselessly finished his task and carefully descended the chapel steps with the help of his cane. Just when he must have been thinking he had the day in the bag and could trot peacefully off to Vespers, he noticed three non-Greek pilgrims in a huddle, eying him with fascination. He looked daunted by the intrusion, but seemed determined to brave it as best he could.

"This is your chance," whispered Charlotte urgently, who might have been listening to my wish after all. Fact is, the cat had my tongue; Greek had Fr. Gregory's. I stood at the heart of a rare, unearthly garden where saints and angels undoubtedly stroll in the cool of the day, and all I could do was panic in the presence of this precious pilgrim of the narrow way. I could not bring myself to ask him to assure me about the three really hard things.

So I asked for a blessing, which he graciously gave. And tossing a quick zing of love our way like a bride's bouquet, Fr. Gregory disappeared into the foliage. I went limp on a nearby bench. The endless sine wave of emotions had taken its toll. Inside-out schedules, clothes that flapped interminably around my ankles, and seven days without a cup of tea had added up. As I remember, someone led me by the hand back to the room.

Later I packed for our 4 a.m. departure the next morning. Storm clouds crowded outside the window and lightening began to rake the sky. The scent of wild, cool wind drew me out onto the covered back porch of the guesthouse to watch a monsoon work its will across the land. Rain lashed at the hot ground, then rose in twisted silver wisps around the stocky bulk of the saguaros. Wind tore crazily at a stand of palm trees and blasted through the neat rows of the monastery citrus orchard.

My life for days had been weighty with strict and scheduled attention to the movement of my soul toward God. Now I felt that circumspect pace unwinding inside as I thirstily drank in the lawless lunacy of the storm, letting the unruly weather buffet me in the dark. I dangled over the porch railing where the warm rain pelted my legs. The storm was setting my inner compass for home.

The monks would be resting in this early evening time, before private prayers started sometime before midnight. Soon the air would fill with their ardent pleas; prayer for their own souls and the souls of countless others. In the privacy of their cells with no one to admire their piety they would wrestle precious human territory from the enemy of humanity out of this world of delusion, bringing sanity and order out of the chaos of sin's ravages across the globe. The sumptuous monastery grounds are a pale metaphor for the unsung work blossoming to fruitful prayer out of the hearts of the monks of St. Anthony's.

A dark figure took shape out of the mist. It was one of the brothers, no doubt completing last-minute duties in the olive grove before his brief sleep period. He strode toward the monks' quarters, in no particular hurry under the heavy rain. As summer cools to autumn the community will harvest their olives, cure the fruit, press the oil. The monks yield to the cycle of the agricultural year as they do to the Church cycles of prayer, fasting and worship. This is the vocation these men were born to. This is an honorable place.

Three days after our return to Denver, Candice called me. She'd been on a short spa getaway with her husband – a perk through his company – and something she'd looked forward to for weeks. At a mountain resort they'd spent two days immersed in herbal body wraps, massages, dinners out; the works.

"I was sitting in the solarium after being pampered all day, wrapped in a spa robe while soft music played over the intercom," she told me. "But I felt lost and a little depressed. The whole thing seemed shallow. I kept wishing I was back at the monasteries with my friends, sweating in the desert and praying through all those services."

I couldn't have agreed more.

CHAPTER 8: Going Under the Mantle

Thou hast gone over unto the life unaging, unto the other world, yet Thou art in truth not far from us, for heaven is closer to us than our own souls.

Akathist to St. John of San Francisco

Nothing compares to the moment when a desire long held materializes to reality. I was finally going to venerate the relics of St. John Maximovitch, after at least seven years of longing. In a way I'd already made the pilgrimage, well before the day I finally decided to book a flight to San Francisco. Early in my pilgrimage into Orthodox faith, I was drawn to a full-length icon of St. John in my parish temple. The icon seemed almost alive when I'd pass by to venerate after services. I was attracted by the eyes; they brimmed with strength and pathos. He pleaded with me from the icon; that I would live well, and for Christ.

Someone had told me early on that we don't have to search too far for the saints who will become our patrons, our favorites, the ones to whom we find ourselves going for comfort and assistance time after time. "The saints find us," was her theory. In my interaction with St. John I had found this true. I had consciously done very little, yet I'd been wooed from an icon. I knew beyond a doubt he wanted me to be part of his team.

Beyond the inexplicable aspects of what might be involved in a saint choosing someone as a friend, there was much about the saint's life that impressed me. Born in late 19th century Russia, St. John had been immersed in Orthodox spirituality from birth and was drawn to the ascetic life very early. He embraced monasticism, and soon demonstrated an extraordinary capacity as a pastor and leader, aptitudes that merged with the miraculous as the years passed. He served as a bishop and finally archbishop for the Russian church in several countries. Everywhere, he was revered and loved. He was known for strict asceticism, deep humility and special concern for children. And intertwining it all, healings and the gift of clear sight.

St. John spent his last years in San Francisco coordinating construction of the new cathedral, Joy of All Who Sorrow. In the end, people mistrusted him; people weaker in faith whose foibles and lack of foresight were visited on his holy nature and broke his heart. Photos of him in later years show a stooped little man in heavy liturgical robes with the look of another world in his face. Though in every picture, he seems to radiate a lively inquisitiveness toward the other person, and a refreshing dearth of ego. It's those eyes.

When this unusual man died suddenly in 1966 at age 70, his body was not embalmed. Miraculously, it did not decompose. This phenomenon occasionally accompanies the death of true saints. The body was not buried, but after the funeral was kept within a crypt under the cathedral whose construction he had faithfully supervised. After his canonization in 1994, the still-incorrupt relics were enshrined in the nave of the church, where they remain today for veneration in a glass-topped sarcophagus.

In the season of my first fascination with this saint, I dreamt I stood at St. John's shrine. Bending over the reliquary, I begged his intercession for a chronic health issue. In the way of dreams, I accepted as a matter of course when the deceased began to speak, assuring me I would be healed and urging me to bring others to him as well. "Bring them all; I'll heal them all," was his emphatic response. I turned to see a door hovering in midair without attachment to walls. In the porous way of dreams I was easily made to understand that this was the door through which others would come to the saint for prayer. The dream evaporated before I could turn the doorknob.

A few years later, my Advent prayers were inspired out of the poignancy of *Prayers by the Lake* by St. Nikolai Velimirovich, personal prayers this Serbian monk had written during a year in midlife at his secluded lakeshore monastery. The prayers were so raw, so honest that it hurt to read them. This monk longed for God above everything. His prayers took me to a new level of exposure to my own longings for a deeper inner life. St. John came constantly to mind as I longed and ached my way through Advent. When quiet Advent approached the Nativity, I knew I should not go another year without a visit to the one who had "gone over unto the life unaging."

I called my childhood friend Julie, booked two of the cheapest flights I'd seen in a decade, and started packing one tiny daypack for the trip. Into it went only a prayer book, a few toiletries and an extra sweater and rain pants against the notoriously changeable San Francisco weather conditions. In the spirit of *podvig*, I left my favorite eye shadow at home. We would travel as the pilgrims of old, we two, in the advent of a new year. In a gesture of my need for his prayers, I prayed the Akathist to St. John several times in the days before the pilgrimage. This was about more than satisfying curiosity. I wanted healing for the wounds of my soul.

In almost a lifetime of deep friendship, Julie and I had never taken a trip together. I have known this beautiful woman since my first day of eighth grade in a new school. That day Julie saved me from the unutterable teenage humiliation of cafeteria solitude by inviting me to eat lunch with her. Our friendship has not abated since that long-ago September lunch hour. The only difference is that now, we don't share a locker.

San Francisco that January weekend was an explosion of pseudo-spring, nothing like the fits of trademark fog and maddening wind we'd been prepared for by numerous websites. Artists' exhibits crowded the parks, people lounged in tee shirts in outdoor cafés and spilled out of bakeries with their faces to the sun. Hedges bloomed hot pink and white.

We had booked our extraordinarily cheap hotel through friends who work for the hotel chain. These lodgings were located in a part of town gray with neglect, the sidewalks awash in litter. An astonishing number of men I took to be possible representatives of the city's renowned homeless population stood listlessly on curbs or huddled asleep in doorways at all hours. Though we are both squeaky-clean suburbanites, neither of us were particularly alarmed by any of this, or even by the substandard hotel room that sported a shower head with attitude and raw electrical wiring that spurted from one wall. We did, however, balk at the blankets on the beds that hearkened out of a Dickens novel slum. "We *have* no more *blankets,*" the mystified Indian manager told us when we requested different ones. We resigned ourselves to spending both nights with the covers thrown back, zipped into our parkas.

After we had unpacked our meager store of travel belongings, it was time to get ready for the moment I had long waited for; Vespers at the Cathedral of Joy of All Who Sorrow in the presence of my precious St. John. We ate excellent noodle soup in a Thai café before picking our way through the ruinous streets of the Tenderloin to the bus stop. It was a long and jolting ride up Geary Boulevard in the short winter dusk.

At the door of the cathedral a strange thought seized me: *Maybe I'll come back later, I need something to eat.* I was already at the bottom of the steps before the absurdity of this impulse struck me; I had just eaten. This blackout was simple stage fright: I might forget my lines in there, or the audience might jeer. I was bewildered at my nervousness, my intense self-consciousness. Wasn't St. John my friend? I marched back up the steps and opened the enormous cathedral doors for Julie.

A candle dangled in my fingers while my eyes adjusted to the obscurity of the dimly lit nave. The hem of my long black skirt was unraveling around the heels of my hiking boots. Then a rush of rich sensory input filled my eyes and the word *deluge* came to mind. *One could drown here,* I thought. Simply put, I am used to venerating a few icons when arriving at church back home because by golly, that's what we have back home: a few icons. This was something else.

Enormous, vivid frescoes by the renowned iconographer Archimandrite Kyprian soared up every wall of the cavernous cathedral for at least three stories, wheeling their golden narratives across the ceiling. Everywhere I looked were scenes from the life of Christ, the apostles and the prophets. On one wall St. Lazarus had just come forth. On another, wise and foolish virgins wrestled with the law of cause and effect. A depiction of the Virgin Mary entering the temple as a child blended upward into the fruition of her faithful choices in the wonder of Pascha morning where an angel perched on an empty tomb with news it seemed he could barely contain.

Church Fathers and hierarchs gazed upon the scene; unimpassioned, reliable, the bedrock crafters of doctrines against which hell itself has never prevailed. Behind us, Christ held out his arms between two parables; the Publican and the Pharisee in their contrasting states of heart, and the ironic story of the humble Widow's Mite, complete with several deliciously grumpy Rich and their Much.

The frescoes were only the beginning. The temple was, quite literally, crammed with saints. Icons on gilded stands, icons mounted against walls and tucked into crannies above reliquaries of gleaming wood. They lined every physical surface as though arm in arm, dozens of everything and everyone, a Who's Who of the greatest people and scenes from Judeo-Christian history. Something like heaven I imagine, where throngs of sparkly-eyed souls marinated in bliss tumble from every corner of that everlasting culture of joy into a breathtaking cantata of adoration of the Holy Trinity, permeating the tiniest molecule of heavenly space.

I didn't know where to begin, much like the happy predicament we'll have in heaven. All the rules I'd learned about which icons to venerate first and exactly how they ought to be venerated dribbled out my ears onto the tile. This was no example for Julie, unacquainted with the ways of Orthodox worship. I had no choice but to make a go of it, moving toward several that looked like likely Exhibit A and B candidates. I was trembling with the atmosphere of the place, all hush and echoes and a very foreign feel.

A nice Russian lady who spoke no English honed in on my ineptness and guided me toward appropriate icons. She was also to be instrumental throughout the evening in showing the two country bumpkins where to stand so as not to be mowed down by the deacons as they censed the back of the nave in a way I was unfamiliar with. I was that lost.

Only a week before, I had dreamt again about being in the presence of St. John's relics. In the dream, his shrine was off in a cozy side chapel of the church where people could spend quality time alone with him. Perhaps we took numbers and waited our turn. In the dream I'd pulled up a chair and chatted away in front of the reliquary.

I hadn't counted on the fact that the shrine of St. John, looming now in real life across the room, is a veritable revolving door of veneration by the parish regulars when the church is open. So much for the little speech I had prepared. So much for throwing myself with abandon across the sepulcher. I may have flown halfway across the country with great expectations, but it didn't take long to realize that I would have to share my personal, private saint with scores of others equally enamored of him.

When the arriving Vespers crowd had thinned out around the shrine I made my move, stepped into the shrine and made a *metania* within an arm's length of one of the dearest people who had ever lived. Then my mind went blank. I waited for inspiration. A line of people formed behind me and I froze with self-consciousness. There was nothing to do but pay my respects quickly to make room for the next person. I touched a small icon to the top of the sepulcher and stepped away.

The services of Vespers and Vigil progressed, a blur of Church Slavonic. I felt the power of God in that grand place. The sheer scope of His authority was everywhere. Afterwards, I tried once again to venerate, and once again a substantial line gathered immediately behind me. Again I briefly and self-consciously expressed my wooden appreciation to the saint, and left the church.

I felt the stark contrast of worlds as Julie and I stepped into the cool evening. Inside an Orthodox temple, everyone and everything – eyes, hearts, bodies –

is focused in one direction and toward one Person. Whether one understands the language used or not, a common understanding permeates. Out on the busy street, I immediately felt that unison of focus broken up, dispersed into the thousands of directions for love, devotion and purpose that are pursued in a world-class city like San Francisco. People passed us on the sidewalk discussing a dozen topics of alleged import. Horns honked, neon blared out the wares of bars and restaurants. Without the disinfecting presence of sunlight, the dank odor of a city in darkness descended into us. Outside the golden womb of the past three hours, we were back in a world that pokes endlessly in countless alleyways of promise, many of them dead-ended.

We had a snack in the only restaurant in the vicinity of our hotel whose windows we could see through clearly. The warm, upscale bistro beckoned from just across a very real yet invisible line that separated social wretchedness from the trendy theatre district, full of chic and cultural snobbery; in its own way as desperate as life in the Tenderloin. The dining room was strung with tiny white lights, a haven of cleanliness and sophistication where an informed and well-dressed clientele murmured above background jazz. The hamburgers were good, and expensive. Sleep in our parkas came quickly.

Outside the hotel the next morning, we confronted an even more dejected crowd than had lined the streets the night before. The quantity of sidewalk debris had increased overnight, including copious pools of vomit that testified to a rough night for the locals. Men who looked neither fed nor necessarily unfed gazed passively at passersby who by some miracle, marched briskly toward purposeful destinations on a Sunday morning. Our bus was precisely on time, and we were whisked once again up Geary Boulevard.

Christ told the woman at the well that those who worship God must do so in spirit and truth. It was hard to remember that while bathed once again in Church Slavonic for several hours. Here the choir did the liturgical work while the laity stood quietly. Without this involvement and without a language I understood, I felt unnecessary to the process, standing there in my place before the icon of the widow and her mite. But I kept my eye on St. John's sepulcher and on the people that lined up in regular waves to venerate.

My spirits drooped as the service progressed. It would appear there would be no let-up at the sepulcher. I'd been so sure about St. John and myself, so sure we were best friends. Now I felt foolish in my crumbling convert fantasies. St. John himself seemed as remote as my surroundings, motionless in his glass-topped sarcophagus. He was a Russian for Russians, venerated in a fresco-lined cathedral where all but one Divine Liturgy a month is performed in Church Slavonic. Outside in the street, people who spoke ordinary English walked through the morning, unwittingly desperate for the Gospel.

For a moment the coast seemed clear. I started to slip up to the shrine. Immediately the predictable line materialized out of the shadows. In my increasing paranoia, I imagined people boring holes in my neck with their pious Russian eyes, aware that I was only Scotch-Irish-Cherokee, coaxing me wordlessly to step smart and step down. Once again, my well-rehearsed litanies vanished. A fistful of counterfeit jewels, mere adolescent dreams, tumbled and rolled to the ground where I could never retrieve them again.

Julie sat peacefully on her bench, devouring St. Matthew out of the New Testament I'd loaned her. Her theatre production company would soon be writing script for a summer tour to Latvia. How convenient that she was immersed that morning in a rich and decidedly Slavic setting with a choir in acoustic perfection as a sensory backdrop. No doubt she was starting to drip in creative juices. She was living up to her end of the deal as well: keeping me company.

The priest emerged through the royal doors with the covered chalice. It was a short line for Communion, a few very young children and a frail older couple. The service ended after a short homily and announcements, all in Russian to the bitter end.

I was ashamed at how anxious I was to cross the border out of that foreign country into a more familiar world. The air on the street was soft, scented with the sun off the sea. Spikes of bright emerald shoved their way through storm drains, and the sun danced its irresistible glory into the day. The heaviness in my heart lifted slightly.

Julie and I split a pastry at a nearby bakery renowned on the internet for its Russian products. Not knowing what else to do for the moment, we wandered back toward the cathedral. I was in California on a perfect fake spring afternoon after all, fool that I was. I crawled back through my motivation to come here in the first place. I had said I wanted to venerate the relics of St. John, to pay my respects. And I'd done that several times over the course of twelve hours. Yet I had to face the fact that I'd wanted something more, something I thought I should have been able to access effortlessly, but obvious hadn't. Something I could not put my finger on.

The door to the cathedral bookstore was open and we went up a flight of stairs and squeezed into the tiny shop packed with titles in both Russian and English, the walls lined with icons. A man named John was behind the counter, obviously not Russian, chatting in English with a friendly Russian-American named Misha. Misha had been baptized by St. John, probably not long before the saint's repose. John conducted the English choir for the once-a-month English liturgy. I explained my interest in St. John, hoping to find in these men some reassurance, some piece to the puzzle.

I wondered aloud why some ethnic churches cling so fiercely to the languages of the old countries, why English has not yet earned the sanctified status of Russian or Greek for some of these jurisdictions, several centuries after the establishment of the Orthodox faith in America. We might discuss this sensitive topic all we wanted, but in the end a perfect expression of the Faith, anywhere and at any time, is probably not possible in this world. The Church as an entity established by Christ, is perfect. The people that make it up – all of us – are not. None of us comes to the table without history, culture, personal taste and limitations of vision. Until a more perfect future day, an ardent forbearance of our fellow Christians and fellow humans will please Christ more than individual rubrics for correctness.

John had a meeting and needed to close the bookstore. I quickly asked for information about the house where St. John had established his Chinese war orphans after World War II, and where he had lived himself during the San Francisco years. Today, the building still houses the parish church of its patron, St. Tikhon. I had gotten only recordings from the phone company for all three of the numbers I'd found on the internet.

According to Misha, there was a pilgrim-friendly priest named Fr. James who served at the Old Cathedral of the Holy Virgin, the original church where St. John had served in the city. This Fr. James liked to host pilgrims on St. John tours around the city. He might be willing to show us the St. Tikhon Home. I brightened at the idea.

We changed out of church clothes and took a couple of lumbering city buses out to Ocean Beach, alive with happy Californians. A Frisbee contest was in process, and some students had sectioned off a small soccer field for a game. Children carved cities in the sand, couples strolled at the water's edge, dogs romped next to their owners. The scene was American, familiar, welcome. We ate deli sandwiches on warm sourdough bread just out of Frisbee range and watched a couple of entertaining dogs, which made Julie miss her own dogs. A group of bouncy teenagers offered each other endless piggyback rides up the beach, and chased each other into the cold surf. I began to miss my kids.

The afternoon sun dropped lower and the air was suddenly chilly in the weakening light. The sand was cold under the plastic bag I sat on. Fighting down despair about the weekend so far, I fished out my cell phone and called the number John had given me for Fr. James. My heart sank when the answering machine came on; this was the church phone, not a private number. Some church offices are closed on Monday. The pilgrim-enjoying Fr. James might not get my message for several days, while we had a mid-afternoon plane to catch the next day.

Surfers in wet suits lay prone on their boards, bobbing among the gentle swells as diamond shots of sunlight made the water glisten around them. They were waiting for the perfect moment, the perfect wave. In the way of the born athlete, they would do this waiting with infinite patience. These young men understand what it costs to obtain the best.

A lean blond teenager was suddenly on his feet. His long-honed instincts had told him the perfect swell was under his board. A graceful curve of smooth green ocean propelled the boy up and forward where momentary freedom was unleashed through his body as he cut a white line diagonally down the wave. Liquid as water, exquisite artistry while the surf roared. "In your patience possess ye your souls..."

Landlocked and dull, I watched from my plastic bag high on the sand. Like the less-experienced surfers, it seemed I couldn't feel the perfect wave when I had it under me. I stared into the sea, aware of the miles between myself and St. John, alone now in the locked cathedral.

Somewhere, I'd lost the pilgrimage. It had slipped through my fingers and the opportunity was gone. Who was I kidding; I was unworthy, overlooked, like I imagine those uncoordinated kids in grade school felt, the ones who were always picked last for teams in gym class.

I was glad to have Julie beside me. She has sat with me in many such moments across the years. There were the dark hours in the hospice room while I clung to my mother's dead body long after everyone else had left. In high school many years before, she had sat with me on her lawn on an October afternoon while I wept out bitter and final acceptance; deathly acceptance that the boy I'd loved fervently from afar for two unrequited years would never, not in a hundred repeats of those years, adore me as I had him.

She hadn't said much at those times and she said little now. I envied her a bit, she who had no perpetual craving to connect on some enigmatical level with the relics of incorrupt archbishops. But as always, she was willing to pursue saints with me, go where the brave dare not go with me; to the ends of the earth if need be.

It had become even colder. We walked the length of the beach against the sunset and caught a bus back to town. At a crowded Mexican restaurant down the street from the cathedral, we ate half-heartedly. The waiter spoke little English. The walls were cluttered with photos of the owner's grandchildren in enormous *sombreros,* myriad autographed soccer teams, and paintings of Madonnas with child riding donkeys into Egypt against black velvet skies.

On Monday, we woke later than we'd planned. The heat I thought I'd turned up at bedtime had actually been the air conditioning, and the room was cold. We shivered into our clothes and I decided to call Fr. James again. I articulated the details of our predicament slowly into the church's answering machine as to a room of Berlitz students.

"I am not expecting any red carpet treatment," I emphasized. "It would be enough if someone would just let us into the house." I could hardly refrain from screaming: *Even so, this is the most important message you have ever or will ever receive. Please respond before drawing another breath.* I snapped the phone shut and a wave of longing washed through me, longing for something rare and wonderful that I felt was at my fingertips yet infinitely outside my grasp.

Suddenly I knew it was imperative we check out of the hotel immediately and catch a bus for St. Tikhon's. We must go without makeup or breakfast or the luxury of hesitation. This burst of resolution surprised me. But Julie, for whom Joyfully Welcoming A Bright New Day is second nature, took the plan in stride. We paid our meager dues to the little Indian man and sprinted to the bus stop. The ride was prettier than any we had taken so far, past the tall, closely-built Victorian homes that characterize San Francisco, crammed with their gingerbread accents and bay-windowed turrets. The sky was again blue and flawless, and come what may, I was going to do everything in my power to visit the place where my hero had lived in this city, where he had kept his small cell and taken what little sleep he indulged in and simply *lived* when not in constant motion with his many administrative duties and charitable works.

It is my nature to idealize what and whom I love. No doubt my life would be less complicated if I were *more* cautious, *less* credulous, *more* realistic, *less* enthusiastic about the people and causes I embrace. But on that January Monday, amendment of my basic temperament was not on the agenda. I was going to revel in naïve idealism and adrenaline rushes to my heart's content. If I could get into the house, that is.

We went boldly through a charming iron gate and up the brick steps of the large house. No one answered our knocks and rings, no matter how many positive thoughts and ultimatum prayers we bored fiercely through the door. Undaunted, we found an unlocked gate on the street that led into an enclosed courtyard next to the house. A mosaic cross graced one end and a small shrine nestled among shrubbery at the other. The courtyard held a mossy, shadowed scent.

In this courtyard St. John had sometimes held services. One was Epiphany, the feast day of the Baptism of the Lord when the waters are blessed for the coming year. Once while St. John's hands were lifted in prayer over the basin of water to be blessed, a white dove soared out of the sky and swirled around the basin.

According to witnesses, the bird soared and descended again and again as St. John continued to pray. It finally alighted on the saint's shoulder, bringing people to tears with this extraordinary coincidence commemorating the manifestation of the Trinity.

Sometime later, St. John tended to a wounded white pigeon he found in the yard. The bird became a sort of pet. Observers believed St. John had very real and mysterious communication with the pigeon. It was as though the bird brought messages from heaven while St. John taught the bird in turn. On the day the saint died, 800 miles away in Seattle, the housekeeper noticed the bird writhing on the window sill where it usually perched, as though in agony. It declined rapidly and died.

Julie wanted pictures of the house, so we crossed the street to get a better view. I called the Old Cathedral again, and a friendly person who identified herself as Mother Maria began to give me careful directions to the church, so I wouldn't miss talking with Father James, she explained. I restrained myself from offering Mother Maria or anyone else a lifetime gift card to Starbucks if they would drop whatever they were doing and proceed swiftly to the current center of the universe – the corner of Balboa and 15th Avenue – with a key to the magic St. Tikhon Home and Church. What *was* it with everybody's fascination with old cathedrals and Fr. James? I'd told these people I wanted no red carpet treatment or fanfare, just a gander at St. John's little cell. Just a key! A key!

An angel driving a mid-sized sedan and wearing a tweed sport coat pulled up in front of the house. Trying not to appear overly wild-eyed, we followed the tweeded angel back through the gate. This was Peter – a human as it turns out – who works for the Archdiocese of the Russian Orthodox Church Abroad and had stopped by St.Tikhon's for something on his way to a meeting. He believed our story about being on the verge of certain expiration if we could not tour the house. He told us to tour to our heart's content during his meeting, but not to touch anything. Afterwards, he would drive us himself to the Old Cathedral, since we absolutely must tour it and meet Fr. James. We gave up and agreed.

In the front hall we slid off our packs. A sleepy-looking young man padded silently out of nowhere to light candles in the chapel to our right, disappearing into the mist as quickly as he'd come. Peter drove away and the house was silent. We were alone in the house of a saint.

Silence is not strong enough a word for the quality of stillness felt in that hall. It seemed impossible in a busy urban neighborhood on the street of a major bus line. It had a life of its own, this stillness. Here with his orphans St. John had held services in the chapel dedicated to St. Tikhon of Zadonsk. On the other side of the hall was a dining room where there had been recent activity, no doubt connected with the old-calendar Christmas festivities of the parish.

I ventured into St. John's cell, a room so small there was no room for a bed. But then, St. John had never lain down to sleep anyway. His pattern was to pray all night and catch a short nap in a sitting position toward morning, his choice when he was tonsured a monk. An old chair sat in one corner, *the* chair where St. John had taken those famous catnaps. Peter had assured us we were welcome to sit on the blessed chair, an apparent exception to the no-touching rule. So I sat in the old yellow chair and wondered about the body chemistry of a person who rarely slept and still managed to become holy, while the rest of us to a man become progressively more horned and fanged without regular sleep.

As to the holy man's personal things arranged on the cluttered shelves, desks and tables of the room; what, after all, did a saint need? A glass bowl of Russian Pascha eggs caught my eye, obviously decorated by children. The Key to The City of San Francisco lay near a fountain pen and ink blotter on the desk, next to an old-fashioned rolling desk calendar that displayed the month and day of my wedding anniversary. Icons, pictures of friends, reverend elders, fellow clergy and perhaps family, covered the walls.

It is true that St. John probably "realized his human potential" more than most of us will. Yet standing there in his small room, it was obvious that he did what every person does every moment of every day: he made choices in light of the best he knew. He chose to pray entire nights. He forgave his enemies. He offered his shoes, his heart, his healing prayers to the sick, destitute and prisoners wherever he happened to find them. Sometimes he arrived late and barefoot to church services because of it. He focused his energies day after day, moment by moment, toward the Source of all life. But he accomplished this incrementally, like everyone else moves themselves one moment at a time ever closer to what he or she will be in the end.

Our angel returned to the house and drove us through steep San Francisco streets to the Old Cathedral of the Holy Virgin on Fulton Street. Hieromonk James Corazza met us at the door, smiling and gregarious. "I'm terrible with names," he announced happily after we introduced ourselves. He immediately asked us to set down our packs and follow him to the back of the nave where we faced the altar.

What was before us was surely a dream. Morning sunlight from a large window above the narthex cast a pool of sunlight onto a polished hardwood floor, the light divided into two pools by a wide, crimson-red carpet runner that ran to the Royal Doors. Like special effects in a movie, polished surfaces of a double-tiered icon screen reflected an improbably gold brilliance, an interplay of paint with light. Incredibly, here were Julie and I, mere stumblers into this beauty. And to think we might have missed it.

A vaulted ceiling of dark timbers – some taken from old sailing vessels – soared upward to meet and clasp high above the icon screen, drawing the eye into obscurity. This contrast of darkness against the brightness of the icon screen extended deeply into the apse, where shadows lit faintly by indigo stained glass filtered into the room in smoky sheaths. Within the blueness of that altar space church parishioners had sometimes found St. John at prayer, aglow with an unearthly light, his feet several inches off the ground. The archbishop finally started locking the altar door behind him so as not to startle people.

Several other pilgrims were present, whispering unobtrusively at one side of the nave with Mother Maria, the nun who had answered the phone earlier. "This church is part of a corridor of sanctity," Mother Maria told me quietly. "It threads its way through the city from this place, to St. Tikhon's, to the New Cathedral. Please tell people that". Her eyes reached into the distance as she spoke.

Fr. James led us all forward to a long drape of faded red satin that hung over a stand in the center of the red carpet. Enveloped in the upper folds of satin was an icon of St. John. "This is his mantle, his *mantiya,*" he told us. My heart began to pound and tears stung my eyes as this piece of information registered. It had not been I after all, who had moved heaven and earth that morning. It had been God. I wasn't an insignificant pest, an annoying shrine loiterer, a lowly speaker of an unworthy language. I was important enough to be standing in a pool of light near a wonder-working mantle that a true saint had left as a holy keepsake for the Faithful on his way to the next world.

Fr. James explained that he would serve a *molieben* to St. John, a short prayer service. Then each of us would kneel with our foreheads against the icon while he covered us in the *mantiya* and prayed. Under this mantle, many had been healed of physical ailments or mental and emotional agonies.

The mantle was surprisingly heavy around my shoulders. The sensation reminded me of my father's muscular hugs when I was little. I wept as Fr. James read prayers from the end of St. John's Akathist, the very ones I had prayed so fervently at home before the trip. Of all wonders, I finally had St. John all to myself.

Joy followed me home. The joy was so untamed, so pervasive that I lived for a few weeks under the cheerful delusion that I was almost incapable of ever saying or doing another corrosive, stupid thing as long as I lived. St. John had met me in a way I could not have explained to anyone, but I felt the full effects.

I could leave the story there. That is, if I wanted to sell something. I could claim my character had been irrevocably altered by those moments under the mantle, and somebody would buy it. It is the human way to desire the effortless fairy tale ending. It is the American one especially. Cause and effect even in spiritual matters are imperative to our notions of success. We want to be sure that Massive Output A will result in Amazing Transformation B, as though the Christian life were something like stock investments or dieting.

It is normal to want to believe that the things to which we've given ourselves are worthy of us. We work hard to be the rainmaker, the savvy person who's doing the right thing at the right time, whatever we may perceive that right thing to be.

But alas, this can so easily deteriorate to pride. And so the St. John glow had to go. A soul left to feed alone out of such giddy memories might begin to measure itself against those who had never gone under a mantle. Which would not be fair, because saints' mantles and friendly priests who will take time out from their work day to wrap you up in one are hard to come by. So it wasn't long before I was returned to life as a mere mortal with all its struggle and inconsistency.

At first I chastised myself that I had let something rare and significant slip away. I wondered what I could have done to sustain the glow longer – prayed more, been more determined? Yet even Moses' aura after the 40 days on Mount Sinai faded with time, and he probably did everything right. So I thanked God for marvels both known and unrecognized out of the San Francisco trip, thanked Him for the way He spoils and pampers such a worm as I, and moved on.

Properly taken, the gives and takes of life teach humility and patience, of which I may be catching a whiff. The contrast of red neon blessings against the 40-watt ones are ordained by a God committed to refining people within an imperfect system. For the time being, that is the way we grow. Yet since my St. John pilgrimage I'm more conscious than ever that someday the ebbs and flows of this present life will cease. All ebbing will one day be stilled, leaving only an eternal surge. Pilgrimage will come to an end, in a place where every day is a day under the mantle.

Martyrs of good hope, who flutter around the Light of Heaven like a flock of white doves, pray to God for us.
St. Nikolai Velimirovich

Postscript

Across the floor of Grace Cathedral, an inlaid pavement labyrinth in the Medieval quadrant pattern spreads its coiled, terra cotta elegance. Inspired by the labyrinth at Chartres, it is composed in the motif that characterized these curiosities in European churches of the era. There is one path for travel in and out, a bundle of compacted curls, a tightly-knit journey for the feet and mind. At Chartres, my eyes had been riveted into the loftiness above. I hadn't sought a treasure at my feet.

There is no scholarly agreement about the absolute religious symbolism of the medieval labyrinth. But common sense suggests that such a feature within a cathedral of the highly religious middle ages would have served as a place where people might get out of the weather to walk through their prayers or meditate on the important themes of life.

Today, swatches of watery gold and indigo light sift through the cathedral's splendid stained glass windows and splash across the gray and white pattern of the labyrinth. Such a setting would have been awe-inspiring to the common medieval person coming in out of his small gray world. Then as now, this feature offers its ritual in a rhythmic plot of hairpin turns where at the center of both life and labyrinth, one might find something to sustain the larger pilgrimage.

When I'd planned my walk through this labyrinth I had absurdly assumed I'd be alone for the exercise. A romantic assumption. My real visit takes place in the real world, where majestic cathedrals are typically full of other people. They are with me today in force, clutching brochures, gazing high into the rose window, snapping photos. I am barely into the first circuit when a little girl in the garb of the fairy princess breaks away from her parents and jaywalks to the maze's center. My mind protests; *you're starting at the wrong end.* I have my rules, based on a nice pamphlet I picked up at the door. I sigh; I am too often the older brother in the story of the prodigal son.

But the little girl is not trying to cheat. She's a child observing the grown-ups around her. Her sense of the maze is as good as mine. Once she has skipped into the labyrinth's center she follows the path from the inside out with solemnity and precision. We meet halfway and take each other in for a moment. She freezes, as if stepping aside on lines or cracks might break her mother's back. Like me, it seems it had not occurred to her she might encounter anyone along the way. I smile and let her pass. She is visibly relieved and moves on carefully, scrupulously following the narrow strip of white stone.

A couple of tourists back absentmindedly into the space as they take in the grandeur of the ceiling. They are unaware that five pilgrims now wind the labyrinth with high notions of spiritual enrichment or self-discovery. One of the pilgrims turns a shoulder inward to avoid a collision with the ceiling gazers, who remain oblivious. A tired-looking walker in a windbreaker with a twisted collar takes his paces on the hairpins at a matter-of-fact gait, the resignation of late middle age pressed deeply into his face. Two women in Tai Chi chic have removed their shoes and advance reverently, hands pressed in prayer. I'm feeling a little claustrophobic, but try to receive the experience as it comes to me as I brush against others on the narrow straits.

The walk is not the test of wits I'd imagined it would be, like the tricky corn mazes with their multiple, dizzying choices my children frequent every autumn. I had expected such a puzzle, based on the grim notion that a labyrinth must represent life exactly. Therefore, it must be rife with confusion and illusion. Instead, this walk is a gentle, soothing monotony. There is no need to think or strategize or compete – just follow the terra-cotta. As soon as I'm dedicated in one direction, the path turns me on a dime to take me the opposite. In a way different from my original expectations, it still simulates the feel of real life. This is the way of obedience to the revealed path.

I reach the six-lobed pattern at the center of the labyrinth, satisfied with this simple, obedient effort. Though the monotonous tracks of life seem more often than not to lead nowhere, this exercise assures me in a quiet way that faithfulness to the task at hand has its reward.

The man with the twisted collar reaches the center. He chooses a lobe and stands with hands in his pockets and head sunk on his chest, waiting for something it would seem. I too am waiting, but without the patience for the meditative pose. I begin my journey outward, a repetition of the same tight turns taken backward. The walk out is refreshingly anticlimactic. I emerge my essential self.

I had long waited for this day at the labyrinth. But the anticipated present has quickly receded to the past. Now what? Someone has said that there are two tragedies in life. One is to lose one's heart's desire; the other is to gain it. Gain may prove more confounding than we bargained for. Learning brings its own complications, and often more questions than answers. And always, hairpin turns.